the fairy realm

being an investigation into an ancient belief

Ronan Coghlan

SKYLIGHT PRESS

© Ronan Coghlan, 2015

First published in Great Britain in 2015 by Skylight Press,
210 Brooklyn Road, Cheltenham, Glos GL51 8EA

Ronan Coghlan has asserted his right to be identified as the author of this work.

Designed and typeset by Rebsie Fairholm
Publisher: Daniel Staniforth
Cover design and photography by Rebsie Fairholm incorporating stock textures from sirius-sdz.deviantart.com

www.skylightpress.co.uk

Printed and bound in Great Britain by Lightning Source, Milton Keynes.

British Library Cataloguing in Publication Data:
A catalogue record for this book is available from the British Library.

ISBN 978-1-908011-90-9

contents

The Fairy Folk: by way of being an Introduction

EOPLE who claim to have seen UFOs, aliens, cryptids or things of a similar nature are usually dismissed as mildly odd by the generality of the public. The same cannot be said for people who believe in fairies, by which I mean not just Tinkerbell types, but gnomes, elves, bogles, pixies and other such creatures. The reason for this is simple. While it is vaguely acceptable that other such strange beings fall into the realm of the adult, belief in fairies has become strictly bound up in the popular mind with the nursery. Say you believe in fairies and you will not only be dubbed eccentric, you will be labelled immature, juvenile and possibly half-witted into the bargain. UFOs and aliens have gained themselves a small niche in the 21st Century paradigm, but fairies are quite definitely out of it.

The human mind seems to be constricted by a sense of what it deems in any given era to be and not to be possible. Each of us has boundaries, beyond which we regard something as utterly impossible. These boundaries are frequently determined by the current social perspective rather than pure logic. If people as a general rule dismiss something as impossible, then we too shall so dismiss it. It seems to be that humanity lives at a collective as well as at an individual level. We shy away from whatever is generally disbelieved by our society. Some of the discoveries of modern science would have been thought beyond the credible in earlier societies and their possibility would, in those times, have been discounted. Perhaps we are unduly hasty to regard something as impossible just because that is the general opinion. General opinions have often been questionable in the past, as any historian will confirm.

And so we come to fairies. Fairies, in the case of beings who are not always but sometimes apprehensible to humans, were widely believed in by our forebears and the dismissal of their existence has arisen on conjectural rather than evidential grounds; it is due to belief in, rather than proof of, their non-existence. In other words, *How do we know they're not there?*

A sceptic might reply that the onus is on us to prove they are. You don't see fairies as you make your way through life as a general rule. If people are to show they possibly exist, it devolves on them to produce evidence. Is any such evidence forthcoming? The statement that they were once widely believed in doesn't count as evidence in itself. Many things which we now know to be erroneous were once widely believed in.

One of the troubles with modern science is that it will not accept anything as a scientific proposition unless it is falsifiable; that is, if you cannot produce the sort of evidence that has some possibility of being overturned, it is not a scientific proposition. Thus, unless you can catch a fairy and bring it along for a scientist to examine, it cannot be considered from a scientific viewpoint. Unfortunately, the only real evidence for encountering fairies is anecdotal and you cannot show an anecdote to be untrue. But just because an anecdote is not falsifiable doesn't mean that its content is actually false – merely that a scientist will say, quite correctly, that it cannot be regarded as proof from the standpoint of modern science.

But stay a second, I hear you cry. *Surely there are no eyewitness accounts of fairies that bear the hallmark of authenticity? Surely such accounts are just old folktales, mouthed by unschooled peasants in taverns in the dim long ago?*

Actually, this is not the case. Many accounts come from modern sources. Although there are only *accounts* of fairies, some of them are surprisingly convincing.

Take, for example, the extraordinary story of Peter Rahm or, to be more precise, that of Mrs Rahm. Said Peter was said to be a clergyman of the Lutheran Church and to have signed a declaration on 12th April 1671 to the effect that the incident I am about to narrate in fact occurred. One night in 1660, there was a knock upon his door. Outside was a troll. Now what exactly is meant by the term *troll* here may not be what the word conjures up to the modern mind. It doesn't necessarily mean a monster that lurks under a bridge with a view to impeding goats. I think *troll* in this case may be accepted simply as meaning "otherworldly being". His wife, said the troll, was giving birth and needed help. Would Mrs Rahm come and do the needful? Mrs Rahm did, while her husband, who presumably did not see himself in the role of accoucheur, remained behind. In due course the baby was delivered and next morning Mrs Rahm found payment in the form of silver chippings.[1]

---

1   This account is taken from Grimm, *Teutonic Mythology.*

Now the story of the human woman who plays midwife to the fairies is a common motif in folklore, but here we have such a story affirmed in a legal document: it appears to have happened. I see no motive for the Rahms' concocting the tale. We must certainly consider that we are here dealing with an historical incident.

Very well, I hear you mutter, *but this all happened a long time ago. If such things do happen and fairies exist, why aren't they seen nowadays?*

Such contemporary sightings have certainly been reported. The novelist Pamela Frankau (1908-67) said that in 1918 she was in her bedroom at Claremont School, Eastbourne, when she saw a diminutive being running across the floor. In the 1960s, fairies dancing around a tree were reported by dwellers on Victoria Road, Colchester. In 1982 two girls watched two entities that looked like gnomes digging a hole in the playing field of Jaywick's Frobisher Primary School at Clacton-on-Sea. A well-known story recorded by Janet Bord states that in 1979 about four children aged 8-10 saw a crowd of little men endowed with long white beards and caps resembling nightcaps driving in small cars around Wollaton Park in Nottingham. The children's accounts were recorded by their headmaster.

As you may imagine, the Internet is not lacking in such stories either. For example, Charlene W., writing to the website *Fairy Gardens*, said her father and his siblings claimed to have played with little people by the riverside. They gurgled, but did not talk.

This is by no means an exhaustive excavation of modern day stories of fairies. One might say it doesn't prove anything regarding the existence of fairies. My point, however, is that it shows there is just as much anecdotal evidence to warrant investigating their existence as there is in looking into such phenomena as extraterrestrials, bigfoot and the Jersey Devil. To this I would add that, while I cannot prove fairies' existence, I can show the *possibility*, nay, even *probability* that they form part of reality.

Some, of course, scorn even the possibility of them, but that doesn't mean they don't exist. People said the okapi didn't exist, that it was merely the subject of African folklore, yet okapis were later found and exhibited in zoos. A scientist shown a dead platypus said such a creature couldn't exist, it had been faked. He tore it apart to find where the joining wires were. A creature with a bird's beak that laid eggs yet suckled its young was a non-starter in the zoology of the day, yet his tearing operation revealed the platypus to be a truly a genuine animal. If you don't believe me, take the next plane to Australia and you'll see them there. Of course, this is not necessary if you're already in Australia.

In fact, it is very hard to prove something doesn't exist. The only way I know is as follows.

You have the situation:

(a) if A exists, B cannot exist
(b) A exists
therefore B does not exist.

No such proposition exists where fairies are concerned. Therefore, they may exist.

But hold! cries one of sceptical bent. *I invoke the Celestial Teapot argument.*

This was produced by Bertrand Russell, who said there could be a teapot, too small for detection, floating about in space. You can't prove it doesn't exist, but no reasonable person would suppose that it does.

What Russell is saying is that some things are patently absurd and you don't need to disprove their existence to know they aren't there. The problem here is that different people have different Absurdity Thresholds. What Jack thinks Absurd, Jill may think Just Possible, while Hezekiah may think it Probable. I daresay most people would agree with Russell about the absurdity of his interplanetary teapot, but there are other things which to certain people might seem less absurd, yet they are beyond the bounds of everyday experience. Is the existence of an alternative race, coexistent with us but generally unperceived by us, in the same bracket as the teapot? It is not so long since nobody realized we shared the world with countless millions of microbes, invisible to us. Had you suggested it, I suspect there would have been many a snort of scorn.

In a time when physics admits the possible existence of other universes, other life-supporting planets, time travel and goodness knows what else, some of which were once regarded as the stuff of science fiction if not pure fantasy, you can't brush aside fairies as a patent absurdity. We are now told by particle physicists that one can move a particle from point A to point B without its travelling over the intervening distance. I shall proffer another example of views in whose absurdity people can mistakenly believe.

Let us take two cavemen, whom we shall call, for the benefit of our example, Ug and Brag, and listen in to their conversation.

Ug: Brag, has it ever occurred to you that the world might not be – er – flat?

Brag: Duh! You can see it's flat with lumpy bits sticking out of it. What an absurd idea! Next you'll be saying it's round like an orange.

Coming to more modern times, the science fiction writer Arthur C. Clarke recalled being told by his mother than in a field nearby there were sheep with four horns each. The young Clarke dismissed this as utterly impossible, the stuff of toddlers' tales, such things were utterly absurd. Shortly thereafter he visited the field and saw the sheep. The present writer has seen this breed of sheep and they certainly look bizarre and otherworldly, but their actual existence is all too verifiable. Clarke had to revise his idea of where the borderland of the Absurd lay.

A friend of mine was telling me he had an acquaintance who lived at times with the pygmies in Africa. These pygmies lived in a dense jungle and had never been beyond it. One day, the acquaintance was summoned out of the jungle and, getting into his vehicle, offered to take one of the pygmies with him. When they quitted the jungle, his diminutive companion probably found it surprising enough. Here were no trees round about. Then the pygmy commented on some ants he could see.

"Those are not ants," said the driver. "Those are antelope in the distance."

The pygmy, who had never seen anything in the distance, scoffed. They were not antelope, he said. They were small. Having grown up in a tree-surrounded locality, he had no concept of distance perspective. When the driver drove to the antelope and showed the pygmy what they were, he was thrown into utter confusion and perhaps distress, for he found the world a very different place from what he had thought it to be. His whole idea of the structure of the world he inhabited had to be reassessed.

In this volume I shall first try to give a general definition of what fairies are and then see if there are any accounts available which might validate their existence. Of course, some alleged sightings may be merely hallucinatory, but, if an account is verified by more than one witness, this is much less likely to be the case. If several persons in different instances report similar phenomena, the phenomena are likelier to be true. There is also the possibility that certain stories are merely fabrications. We have to study all accounts to assess the likelihood of their veracity. But we should not discount the possibility of a story's truth merely because it seems unlikely.

This having been said, there will always be some who will say, *Such and such* cannot *exist*. But people such as they would have said in the past that certain things we know to be true today just *could not* be true. The story of the tropical natives who scoffed at the notion of ice, because solid water *could not be* shows how something totally foreign to our experience can so easily beget incredulity.

I would ask the reader to keep an open mind on the possibility of fairy existence, no matter how hard he may find it, and to judge the arguments and evidence I will present him with as dispassionately as he can, no matter how absurd some of them may seem. This is not a work that seeks to prove the existence of fairies, but it is one that tries to present evidence of their possible existence.

Origin of the word "Fairy"

In classical mythology there were three goddesses referred to as the Fates, who had power over the destiny of gods and men. They were called Clotho, Lachesis and Atropos. For each man, Clotho spun the thread of life, Lachesis measured it and Atropos cut it. They wore white.

Their name in Latin was *Fatae*, from which Italian *fata*, Spanish *hada* and ultimately French *fée* and English *fay, fairy* are thought to be derived. Other sources have been suggested, but this seems to me to be the most convincing.

Fairy and Faerie

Both spellings seem to be acceptable in usage today. However, historically, *fairy* means the actual being and *faerie* the land of the fairies or enchantment generally. I have therefore selected the first of these spellings.

Paracelsus

As the medieval era was drawing to a close, there appeared a scientist who studied *inter alia* the fairy realm. This was Philippus Aureolus Theophrastus Bombastus von Hohenheim (1493-1541). Happily for all concerned, he wrote under the name of *Paracelsus*. He averred that the elements had spirits which occupied them – *sylphs* in the air, *gnomes* in the earth, *undines* (water) and *salamanders* (fire). He is, in fact, the inventor of the word *gnome*.

Chapter One

what are fairies?

BEFORE we look into the possibility of their existence, it might be no bad idea to define what exactly fairies are. The image conjured up in many minds is that of the fairy of book illustrators, a flying female dressed as though about to perform in the ballet and waving a wand. As far as this book goes, it is my intention to cover a wider field. Elves, knockers, goblins, brownies, lutins and even those dread creatures of the fairy tale, the giant and ogre, will feature. I shall keep generally within the field of European beliefs, including those of European origin in lands beyond, not because of eurocentric prejudices, but simply with a view to keeping the book within a reasonable length. However, the odd non-European being who has fallen within the belief systems of colonial populations has been treated. In other words, otherworldly beings amongst the descendants of immigrants to America and other such countries will be included.

Fairies are generally conceived as beings who are supposed to share the world with us, but usually keep out of our sight. They may regard the human race as potentially dangerous, though I cannot see how they might have formed such an opinion. That last remark was intentional sarcasm, by the way. The human race has, in the past, shown a woeful propensity for destruction and harm.

The ancient Greeks believed in nature spirits called *daemons*. These should not become confused with the modern word demons, although the latter is derived from the former. Many kinds of fairy would have been considered daemons by the ancient Greeks, by no means all of them wicked. The term fairies has, in the past, been used to cover nature beings, local beings and beings that were once, but are no longer, revered as gods. I use the word *being* in preference to *spirit*, because the latter has definitely no physical composition, while the former may have. There are certainly kinds of fairy that may be called "lordly fairies" – tall and regal. Sometimes they ride about on horseback and are termed Trooping Fairies. It is at these we shall look first. Doing research in Leitrim (Ireland), D.L. Leland pointed out that fairies there were regarded as being of human size, but capable of shape shifting.[2]

Fairies and Gods

Some beings, regarded latterly as fairies, were once revered as gods. These, I feel, may have been beings of a race higher up the line of being than humans in their powers, but in reality not gods. They often showed all-too ungodlike weaknesses. The novelist Mark Chadbourn features them as powerful beings who, while not being gods, were only too happy to let the human race believe they were. This is how I would regard them.

We shall start in Western Europe, in Ireland. In prehistoric Ireland there was a race of beings called the Tuatha Dé Danaan, the folk of the goddess Dana. Dana was sometimes called Anu (? mother) and seems to have had her beginnings amongst the Continental Celts as a river goddess (the Danube probably took its name from her). In Ireland, however, she was a goddess of the earth. Her other name was the Morrigan, which means great or phantasmal queen, and in this guise she was a war-goddess. She was the consort of the chief god, the Dagda (good god) who had the name Eochaid Ollathair (Great Father). He had a number of other names which seem to identify him with the sun, such as Aedh (fire) and Derg (red). When Christianity supplanted paganism, instead of saying these beings never existed, it was said they had gone into the *sí* or burial mounds after the coming of the Celts, and that they had been a race not of gods, but of wizards. They were depicted as living in various fairylands such as Tir na nÓg and Emhain Abhlach, as well as beneath the *sí*. As these were somewhat paradisal realms, the question arises whether the Irish considered the *sí* as merely portals to them. The term *sí* (pronounced *shee*) came to be applied to the fairies themselves. The idea that it is connected with Gaelic *sith*, 'peace', is a mistake.

So it was that the gods of ancient Erin became a major fairy race. There seems to be some doubt about whether the Irish had believed in a fairy race before this and that, when Christianity arrived, they amalgamated it with the race of gods. Later writings made Bodb Derg the king of the Tuatha Dé, but their original king had been Nuada

---

2   *Folk-Lore,* Volume 7, No.2.

(? fisher). They had the power of invisibility and were of normal human size. Indeed, they could interbreed with humans.

This pantheon of gods was widespread amongst the Celts. In Britain, for example, Dana was Dôn, while in her guise as the Morrigan she seems to be Matrona, who in later Welsh was called Modron. This goddess was also known amongst the Continental Celts, where she was the deity of the Marne. In her we seem also to have the medieval Morgan La Fée of Arthurian romance, the change from Modron to Morgan appearing to have been made in Brittany. That Morgan La Fée was originally a goddess is attested by various medieval references to her as *goddess, dea phantastica* and *déesse*. In Wales the fairy race after the inception of Christianity came to be known as the Tylwyth Teg, the Fair Folk, said to be fair-haired and beauteous. Their king, Gwyn ap Nudd, is essentially in origin a Celtic god, derived from a deity called *Vindos* (white one). His father Nudd is derived from the god Nodens, who would seem to be identical with the Irish Nuada and who may well be the prototype of the Fisher King of medieval Grail romance. Again one might ask if the gods were amalgamated with a separate, earlier fairy race.

Fairies that were originally gods were also found on the Continent. Germany boasts a number of beings in its folklore who may well be derived from the ancient gods of the Teutons. One is Holda, who turns up in Grimms' *Fairy Tales* as Frau Holle. Holda was said to make a progress around the country between Christmas and Epiphany. Although she could appear in beauteous form, she might also assume the likeness of a crone with a long nose and big teeth. She was connected with spinning and gave presents of spindles; she was associated with the wilderness and wild animals; it was said that when snow fell, Holda was making her bed; women who bathed in her pool in the Messner became healthy and fertile; she had a train of women who rode with her; she seems to have had agricultural concerns. A late Icelandic saga speaks of a sorceress called Hulda, of whom Odin was enamoured. A Huldra, queen of the mountain folk features in Scandinavian lore. The *huldufolk*, Icelandic elves, seem to derive their name from her.

A rather similar being who, despite the reservations of linguists, seems to be much the same as Holda, is Berchta (from Old High German *beraht*, bright), also called Perchta. She was popular in the southern reaches of Germany and also in Switzerland, Austria and Alsace. She would make her annual progress at the time of Epiphany. On that day, a special food had to be eaten. Depending on where you lived, it had to consist of gruel and fish or *zemett*, which was a mixture of flour, milk and water baked in a pan. She was interested in agriculture and would plough underground while her servants, the *heimchen*, would water the fields above. These *heimchen* were small beings. On Austrian holidays today, people dressed as Perchta and a male counterpart, Percht, make their appearance.

That Holda and Berchta were identical seems fairly clear. In fact, in one part of Germany they had a counterpart named Hildaberta. In the 19ᵗʰ Century and perhaps even today, Hyldemoer or Hyderquinde with her attendants lives under the Elder Tree. Frau Harke was another personage of the same nature. The Straggle was said to tease maids who spun insufficiently. As Holda was closely connected with spinning, she may well be Holda with an alternative name.

I suspect a powerful single deity lay behind these characters: the lore about her is now fragmentary.

Similarly, gods have been reduced to fairy status in Italy. C.G. Leland, in the 19ᵗʰ Century, reports continued veneration of the Etruscan gods *Tinia, Aplu* and *Faflon* (originally *Fufluns*) as *folletti* (fairies).

The Lapps/Saami regard a being called Luot-Chozjik as a protectress of their reindeer. She too I suspect was originally paid divine honours.

In Slavic mythology one of the chief gods was Bielobog, the White God. In modern folklore, he has become a helpful being called Bylun, who looks like an old man.

However, some folklorists contend that even in pagan times a fairy host was believed in alongside the gods and, when Christianity became prevalent, their numbers were buttressed by an influx of gods; but they were always believed to be there. An alternative explanation is that there may once have been, and possibly still are, powerful psychic entities of whom science knows nothing, but who were assumed to be gods by our remote ancestors, and fairies by our more proximate ones.

Elves and Dwarfs [3]

Elves and dwarfs are, in many ways, the two main species of the fairy clan. They come from Germanic belief. Indeed, in certain works, elf is used for the male of this species, fay for the female. There is also an English word *elfin* for a female elf, but it is rarely to be met with. Grimm averred all elves were male. A certain kinship exists between elf

---

3   The correct plural of *dwarf* is *dwarfs*; Tolkien uses *dwarves*, which he felt less effete, and this plural is now gaining a certain currency.

and dwarf, as dwarfs sometimes bore elfish names (e.g. *Alfr, Gandâlfr, Vindâlfr*). As to their size, Grimm tells us that humans were bigger than elves to the extent that giants were bigger than humans. However, Tolkien is convinced that elves were originally of human size. There seem to have been three kinds of elf in Germanic lore: Light Elves, Dark Elves and Black Elves. (The latter may be identical with the dwarfs). The touch of an elf, even the touch of his breath, could bring sickness. Elves are tricksters when it comes to dealing with the human race. They can vanish. They are fond of music and there are many accounts of the Little People dancing. It is said in Sweden that the mountain elves (*bergfolk*) can dance at night until cockcrow, but not after, or they will become frozen, but invisible. Elves and humans can interbreed. A well-known folk story tells how an elf maid sees a knight on his wedding day and leads him into the realm of the elves. The elves let him go and he thinks he has been away only a short time, but it turns out that his sojourn has been forty years. In Denmark, elves are ruled by kings, one of them said to be at Möen (Kongsbjerg). His queen is very beautiful and lives at the Queen's Chair (Dronningstolen). Another elf-king called Stevne. Grap, elf-ruler of Rügen, is their enemy. An alternative tradition speaks of a single king ruling in all these areas. King Tolv is said to rule at Sjelskör, Sjaelland. There have been tales of the elf-king of Bornholm's musicians playing on fife and drum. Oak trees at the churchyard of Stove Haddinge (Sjaelland) are said to become the elf king's soldiers in the night-time. The elf-king of Stevne has a bedroom in the church wall. On the island of Bornholm, there are military elves.

The Dutch *stallkarl* is regarded as an elf who lives in a stall. The hills under which elves live can be elevated on red pillars, so you can see what is underneath. Lime trees are popular with elves.

Intermediate between elves and humans were the *hogfolk*, who lived in the hills. Feasts of *alvermen* are said to occur in Flanders. Join them and there you will be for all time, unless you ask someone to pass the salt.

Dwarfs may originally not have been small, but by the time Snow White visited them their stature was smaller than that of humans. They seem to have been generally regarded as rougher looking than the elves, with less elegant clothing. They were ill-shaped and hunchbacked. They were grown by the age of three. By the age of seven, each was endowed with a grey beard. Sometimes their feet were said to resemble those of a goose or duck. They would on occasion abduct maidens. They had kings with names such as Goldemar and Sinnels.

They had powerful caps or cloaks, which enabled them to become invisible. In Germany the term *earthman* was sometimes applied to them. On Rügen they believed in three kinds of dwarf: White Dwarfs who were gentle and lived above ground in summertime, who were craftsmen in gold and silver; Brown Dwarfs, who did not exceed 18" in height, had caps of invisibility, were shape-shifters and also craftsmen in gold and silver; and Black Dwarfs, who were the size of a three-year old child, grey in colour and of geriatric appearance. Their clothing was formed of moss. Trolls are sometimes, but not always, dwarfs. They may at times be regarded as gigantic.

These Teutonic creatures were probably introduced to England by the Anglo-Saxons, who invaded in the 5th Century. At first the word *alp* was used for a fairy generally.

In Italy the *ice dwarfs* were said to inhabit tunnels in glaciers. The dwarfs in the Dolomites had a king called Laurin. Dwarfs (*nains*) are also known in Breton folklore.

Nature Fairies

These are the fairies that inhabit or preside over trees, woods, mountains, streams and the like. The Greek nymphs are notable here. There were categories of nymphs presiding over various natural features. In modern Greece the term *nymph* has been replaced by that of *nereid*, which originally meant a sea-nymph.

The nereids of modern Greece are always young and beautiful, though sometimes said to have the feet of goat or ass. J.C. Lawson, writing in the early 20th Century, said he was once in a village where people claimed to know certain nereids by sight. A guide once pointed out a nereid to Lawson, who saw something that looked like a female figure, draped in white and taller than a human, in an olive grove.[4]

In Greek Macedonia (as distinct from the Former Yugoslav Republic of Macedonia) G. Abbott[5] spoke of nature spirits called *drymiais*, who he suggested were a combination of the nymphs anciently called dryads and naiads. He also said that if you spoke to a nereid, you would lose your voice. He said he was not clear whether tree spirit nymphs were said to live in trees, animate trees or simply take shelter in them.

---

4   J.C. Lawson, *Modern Greek Folklore and Ancient Greek Religion* (Cambridge, 1910), p.131.
5   G. Abbott, *Macedonian Folklore* (Cambridge, 1903), p.63.

Pixies

The origin of this word is unknown. In Cornwall it is pronounced *pisky*, but the Cornish antiquarian, Henry Jenner, says, albeit with some reluctance, that the Devon pronunciation of *pixy* is likely to be the correct one. Pixies are as high as a hand and they have either straw hats or red caps. They ride horses and bring them back utterly tired out. They are ruled by a king. The mother of folklorist Theo Brown claimed to have seen pixies when walking around the cliffs surrounding Watcombe Bay (Devon). A friend of the same folklorist saw them regularly on Dartmoor.

The term *pixy-led* is used to describe a situation where you are in a field by night and cannot find the way out. The remedy is to turn your over garment inside out. Although this is an English term, the idea is found at least as far east as Slovenia.

Fairies as the Dead

There are various stories of people seeing those they knew or thought to be dead when they visit the fairy realm. In some cases these are not dead people, but people taken by the fairies, who would have left their body (or a facsimile of it) on a supposed death bed. Some people believed they were dead people taken before it was their time to die and they had to live out their allotted time amongst the fairies.

In the first case, we are not dealing with truly dead persons. In the second, the persons seen appear to be ghosts, but this does not mean that all fairies were so regarded. Fairies and the dead were both considered as living in other realms or dimensions and at times the two could easily become confused.

D.L. Leland, again writing about the folklore of Leitrim, said it was believed that if you actually saw a person who had been taken by the fairies, you could rescue him by throwing over him a mixture of strong urine and hen droppings. What fun, I hear you say.

Homesprites

This is the classification given to fairies who live in and look after the home. In some cases their attachment is to the family who live in the home rather than the house itself. The *brownie* of the Lowland Scots and the *hob* of England are perhaps the best known. The *tomte* is to be found in Scandinavia, as are the *nis* and *nisse*. There is even one type who specialises in looking after churches, the *Church Grim*. The *niss-puki* is a homecarer found in the north of Germany. It has a big head and long arms. The *niagrusar* is the homesprite of the Faroes. It has been suggested that these were ancestors of the family worshipped as gods, but this is only hypothesis.

Homesprites were not unknown among the Slavs either and their ancestral character is found in their name *ded*, grandfather. Some like to take up residence behind the oven, an understandable thing to do if you live in Russia. A usual name for such beings was *domovoy* (lord of the house).

Duendes

The *duende* was originally a homesprite, called in Spanish *duende de casa* (lord of the house). However, in Spain, Portugal, Latin America, the Philippines, Belize and Guam, it is now used to signify quite a wide variety of preternatural beings. It is perhaps best to translate it as *gnome*.

However, it has been used for so many kinds of beings that it would be unwise to speak of a typical duende. For example, Don Campbell encountered Mexican duendes in Chiapas. The males were about 4' tall, the females perhaps 3'8". They looked like hairy humans, the hair being mostly black, but some was reddish brown. [*Fortean Times*: 253]

Evil Fairies

Various fairy types are regarded as downright malevolent. These include bugbears, bogles, bogies and boogers. The term *goblin* is often used for small misshapen humanoids. These are usually, but not always, of an unpleasant nature. On the other hand, the *hobgoblin* is not considered bad at all.

Diminutive Beings

Perhaps the most famous of these is the Irish leprechaun, nowadays a solitary figure, but in earlier times a gregarious soul with abilities to breathe under water. We may add here such creatures as the Sardinian *giane*, the Poitevin *fadet* and even the Little Red Men of Tennessee.

Homesprites such as brownies were often diminutive. The Dutch believed in *kabouters,* one of whose kings lived in a village called Hoogeloon, but was killed by a hunter, so the kabouters left that part of the country. Diminutive beings may often equate exactly to the *daemons* of classical writers.

Mine Fairies

Fairies in mines seem to be beneficial. In Cornwall they are called *knockers,* while in the United States this word has been expanded to *tommyknockers.* The Welsh mine fairies are *coblynau.* In England there are fairies or ghosts that appear as blue flames and are called *bluecaps.* In the south of Germany dwelt the *Wichtlein,* mine fairies who looked like old men with long beards. A mine fairy called Cutty Soames would help the girls in the mines to pull the heavy coal tubs along the rails. In Italy, dwarfs in mines were called *ometti.*

Water Fairies

The mermaid ranks chief amongst these, together with her male counterpart, the merman. The selkie, who has a human form beneath its seal costume, and the Finfolk of Orkney and Shetland should not be overlooked. In Greece, the term *nereid* was used for a sea-nymph in ancient times, but is now used for nymphs of every kind. Eastern Europe has the *rusalka,* the *vodyany* and the *vodnik.* For Germany there is the *nix,* in Scandinavia the *strömkarl.* The latter lived under small waterfalls. In Brittany there is the *morgen.* The *merewiper* (water maids) were said to occupy German rivers. The *neck, nokke* or *nickel* looked like a handsome boy or a man in its upper parts and below like a horse. A mischievous river spirit is the Scottish horselike *kelpie* which will lure the unwary traveller onto its back and then dive into the water with him. The Finnish *vedenhaltia* is a water-spirit. In Poland you have riverbank nymphs called *bokinis* who left changelings and seem to have been the focus of some kind of cult. In Poland and Germany the *waterman* and *waterwoman* were believed in. They resembled humans, though the male of the species was ugly. The Basque *lamia* should not be confused with the character Lamia in classical mythology. They are river-dwelling nymphs. In Spain also you find the *Mozas del Agua,* while in the River Ebro the *Hechiceros del Ebro* are said to dwell.

Cellar Fairies

The German *biersal* lives in the cellar and keeps the vessels clean, for which he is paid a daily jug of beer. The Irish *cluricaun* is also found in the cellar, but he may be just a leprechaun under another name.

Goat Fairies

Amongst these we should place the fauns, urisks of Scotland and other creatures half-man and half-goat reported from various locations. As is well known, the god Pan was half-man, half-goat, but the Greeks in antiquity believed in a whole species of pans. Satyrs were not originally goat-fairies, but became so, in imitation of the fauns.

Gremlins

These are a product of modern imagination, dating from the 1920s. The earliest appearance of the word in print was in 1929. They are blamed for any defects in machinery. At first this was only aeronautical machinery, but now it applies to machinery of any stamp. Gremlins vary from 6" to 2' in height and some have horns. It has been said they have helped pilots to land aeroplanes which are in difficulty. J. Stefko[6] says pilots have actually seen misty shapes aboard their craft. Are these gremlins? In the United States the term *fifinella* has come to be used for a female gremlin.

Giants, Ogres and Trolls

These are, of course, widely found throughout legends and we will look into the various traditions of large wildmen which may correspond to stories of the Bigfoot of North America and the Yeti of the lofty Himalayas. The term *trolls* may apply to a number of different kinds of being. Some are large, like giants, some are small.

In the Orkney and Shetland Islands, off the north coast of Scotland, they believe in diminutive beings called *trows*. This word is a corruption of *troll*. They are found both on land and in the water.

---

6   suite101.com

Hags

Hags may seem a peculiar category to put in a catalogue of fairy types, but hags with magical powers turn up in many fairy stories. The term hag has generally preternatural connections and is related to German *hexe* (witch). In Irish legends we have the *Cailleach Beara*, the Hag of Beare, a peninsula in Kerry. This Irish word for a hag comes from *caille*, 'veil', from Latin *pallium*, and it originally meant a nun, veiled one. Therefore, its application to the Hag of Beare and similar beings must have been comparatively late. The Scottish *Cailleach Bheur* seems to have been a goddess of winter in origin.

In Slavic myth we have *Baba Yaga*, who lives in a hut that has neither door nor window. Ingress and egress are through the chimney. Her cottage is supported by the legs of chickens. She definitely comes into the preternatural class, flying about in a mortar. Romania, which is not basically a Slavic country, has a hag called Mama Padura. She featured in a tale reminiscent of *Hansel and Gretel*. Also found in Romania is Baba Dochia, who was probably a goddess of Spring in origin.

The *Sea-Hag* of Connecticut legend, who is supposed to haunt New Haven, is said to be the ghost of a girl named Molly.

Fairy Rings

These are found in field and forest and, since at least the Middle Ages, have been attributed to the dancing of fairy beings. Unfortunately, this is unsupported by science. Sometimes the grass in them is lush, sometimes it is withered, but it is always ascribable to underground fungi, sometimes manifesting itself in rings of toadstools. Rings in fields are called free fairy rings; rings in woods are called tethered.

Reports of dancing fairies often have them dancing in a circle.

Changelings

It was often believed that fairies would steal babies, leaving ugly or deformed babies in their place. There were sundry stratagems used to prevent this. It is probable that many a child that was merely deformed was regarded as a changeling. Even children who were weakly or ill may have been considered to have been left by the fairies in lieu of some sturdier offspring. It was often thought the fairies could only seize such a child if he were unbaptised. Sir John Rhŷs met a man called Morris Hughes who said he had known someone in Wales who was supposed to be a changeling. This was Thomas Williams of Bryn Syllty, who had been a "sharp, small man, afraid of nothing."

Evans-Wentz mentions the case of a woman in Dinard who was the size of a ten-year-old child, even though an adult. She was regarded locally as a changeling.

In the region of Asturias in Spain, you have fairies called *xanas*. They are small or slim, but cannot provide breast-milk for their offspring (*xaninos*) so they exchange them for human babies.

Tylwyth Teg

These are the Welsh fairies. Some seem to be of human size, while there are two diminutive varieties. In some places they are small thievish folk, living in fern bushes in the mountains and in the winter living in heather and gorse. A slightly bigger variety would carry off unbaptised children.

Miscellaneous

This covers a multitude of creatures, ranging from the *lutins* of Brittany to the *brollachan* of Scotland. More modern creatures are *Mothman* and the *Jersey Devil*. One might even throw in the Scarecrow, as they are said to come alive at night. A glossary of European fairy species can be found in Appendix Two on page 160. However, I have not included werewolves and vampires, as there is already considerable literature on those creatures on the market. Also, while the term *fairy* is used rather loosely in this work, it is stretching it somewhat to include these creatures.

Motifs

There are a number of common *motifs* in fairy stories that seem to recur. One is the story of the woman who is called on to deliver a fairy baby, as in the case of Pastor Rahm's wife given above. However, it has been suggested that human women are called in only when the woman in childbirth is a human whom the fairies have abducted. This might account for occasional real incidents of this nature, which became the stuff of folklore.

Another *motif* is that of the fairy marriage in which a human marries a fairy, but is given a prohibition which, if he breaks it, will result in the fairy's departure. The culmination of the story is that he breaks the prohibition, often by accident.

A third concerns humans who venture into the fairy realm. They find, when they come back after a short time, that many years, perhaps generations, have passed while they were away. The interesting idea that the fairy world and our world have different times is a topic to which we shall return.

Motifs such as these are widespread and probably owe much of this to diffusion, as travelling storytellers went from place to place and sometimes adapted stories to local situations. However, that does not mean the original stories were necessarily fabricated or that similar scenarios were not played out in fact more than once.

The purpose of this book is to study reports which may indicate whether fairies have an objective existence or are merely fictitious creatures dreamed up when people had no other entertainment than a good story to round off the day. As to whether such an endeavour is pure folly, I refer you to the Introduction which, like many an Introduction, has possibly been skipped.

Fairies as Ufonauts

A modern suggestion is that fairies are identical with the alleged inhabitants of UFOs, who have changed their appearance to fit in with modern concepts. Although it is true that both fairies and ufonauts are the subject of sightings, why the ufonauts, whose interaction with humans is supposedly limited, should want to accommodate themselves to modern human culture by changing from their fairy appearance is difficult to guess. Moreover, if these beings have changed their guise from fairies to ufonauts, there should not be any further appearances of fairies, yet there are. Ufonauts have not yielded place to fairies: both are still reported.

Chapter Two
eaRLy HistoRIcaL accounts

E will look first at accounts taken from historical sources. This is not meant to be an exhaustive overview, but merely a list of accounts which have some evidence to back them up or are at least particularly interesting in some other way. Accounts taken from history, particularly in the long ago, are apt to convince the reader less than accounts from contemporary sources.

Archbishop Agobard of Lyons (died 840) wrote a number of works which were lost, but rediscovered and published in 1605. He relates that people in his diocese believed in a land in the sky called Magonia and that its inhabitants in ships used to come to the earth to collect destroyed crops. On earth certain wizards (*tempestarii*) would conjure up storms to destroy the crops and receive some form of payment from the Magonians. Once Agobard was faced by a mob who wanted to stone to death three men and a woman who, they averred, had fallen out of a Magonian ship. Agobard didn't believe a word of it and saved the lives of these unfortunates. He does not seem to have investigated their provenance further. Yet it must be asked why the locals thought they had come from a fairytale land in the sky. Some have thought they might have been extraterrestrial space-travellers, but they seem to have looked human. Not a tentacle in sight.

They may just have been travellers, who tend to be regarded with suspicion by rural communities. But they may have been something else. We have here a reference to four people who were at least considered to be otherworldly beings.

In 1125, witnesses at Railbach, Germany, saw a man who appeared to be composed of fire, with fire issuing from his nose and mouth. What exactly this was I cannot say, but presumably it was not merely some unfortunate who had set himself alight. He was seen again on a couple of occasions, so I think we can discount this unhappy possibility.

While fairies were widely believed in in the Middle Ages, a well-known account was one given to Giraldus Cambrensis (1146-1253;

dates approximate). A man of Welsh princely blood, Gerald was an ecclesiastic, the author of several books. In 1188 he travelled through Wales and here he came upon the following tale. The events in this story occurred shortly before his time. They were narrated by the priest Elidor to David, a Welsh bishop.

To avoid a schoolmaster, Elidor, as a boy, had hidden beneath a bank. After two days he was growing on the hungry side, when two little men approached him. They led him along a path which seemed to be underground and they emerged into a sunlit land, a verdant country: but at night it was very dark, as it had neither moon nor stars. Elidor was introduced to the King. The people seemed to have no religion, but worshipped truth alone. They ate neither flesh nor fish, but subsisted on dishes of milk and saffron. He returned to his mother from time to time by sundry ways and once she asked him to bring her something from this strange land. He stole a golden ball, but could never find his way back to the country afterwards.

This story seems to have been related to Giraldus as both true and recent. Just who told it to him is not clear. If Elidor had never told it, it would have been easily confuted. Did Elidor make the story up? Impossible to say, but he seems to have told it to the Bishop more than once while his tears flowed freely in regret and it hardly reflects much credit on him.

Assuming – and I know it is an assumption that will make many a reader balk – that there is truth in this, where might Elidor have gone? Another dimension would seem to be indicated, as it was a green and pleasant land, but seemed to have decidedly less sunlight than the earth, but not no sunlight at all. Furthermore, the lack of moon and star would indicate that we are somewhere else. It is perhaps interesting to note that the inhabitants seem to have been white and lactose tolerant. These are not particularly old features of the human race. Could there have been a wormhole or portal in Wales? If so, is it still there?

It is at this stage I feel we might mention the Wild Hunt, as we have a supposed actual sighting in the 12th Century. Belief in this seems to be found all over Western Europe and may be part of an original primitive mythology. It is supposed to be the sound of a band of riders thundering through the skies, dressed as huntsmen or warriors, horsed and with the music of hounds accompanying them. Whether we can regard its frenetic riders as *fairies* I know not, but we can certainly classify them as *preternatural beings*.

Its original leader may in fact have been the god Woden (=Scandinavian *Odin*) as he is frequently described on the Continent as the leader and it is appropriate that he led a warband, for he is called in the *Ynglinga Saga* the inventor of war. His name is thought to signify some sort of frenzy. However, he may have taken over from some older leader, whose name is lost in the mists of antiquity.

A sighting of the Hunt is supposed to have occurred in England in 1172. According to the *Peterborough Chronicle*, the new abbot, Henry of Poitiers, did not meet with the chronicler's approval and he informs us that, after his appointment, hunters blowing horns were seen at night by many, accompanied by hounds. They were black, fearsome and loathsome and were both in the deer park and in the town of Peterborough. It was claimed there were twenty or thirty reliable witnesses. It has been suggested that these were not real wild hunters, but persons not numbered amongst the abbot's fan club in disguise. Another manifestation is alleged to have occurred in the 17th Century, when there was an earthquake in Wiltshire. The antiquarian John Aubrey says many reliable people heard the sound of the hounds in the air. A Mr Holland, who wrote in 1861, said he had heard hounds overhead in the sky as he passed a church in Sheffield on a dark night. This shows for how long the notion of a hunt in the sky continued in folk belief. We shall be hearing more of the Wild Hunt when we devote a chapter to it.

Another account which I am about to give is very well known and has been used before as evidence for the existence of fairies. That is the story of the Green Children of Woolpits. This is set in England in the reign of King Stephen (1135-54), but it may have occurred a little later. It is attested by two writers, Ralph of Coggeshall (died around 1227) and William of Newburgh (12th Century), who said there were many credible witnesses to the events. Two green children, a boy and a girl, in strange garb and unable to speak English were found near St Marys of the Woolpits in Suffolk. They were taken to Sir Richard de Calne (died 1188 or earlier). The boy died, but the girl grew and learned English. Her green colour in due course faded.

She said they came from a land where all things were green and the light was dim. They had followed their father's animals into a cavern and come out by another entrance, lured by the tinkling of bells. On emerging, they were struck senseless by the sunlight, brighter than anything they were used to. The land they came from was called St Martin's Land.

They may, in fact, have been the children of Flemish immigrants living near Fornham St Martin. Flemings had been persecuted in the reign of Stephen's successor, Henry II, and they may have been hiding in the woods, the dim sunlight imbuing everything with a greenish hue. The skin of the children may have been affected by malnutrition, which can induce chlorosis.

However, one accepts this explanation with caution. In the reign of Henry II, the incident would have been later than the records state. The children would eat only beans, which sounds a little strange. Generally, children will show reservations about strange food, but, if they were ordinary humans, surely staples such as bread and milk would have been familiar to them. While the present writer regards the Flemish explanation as possible, he does not treat it as absolute certainty.

A similar story, set in a village called Banjos in Catalonia in the 19th Century, is a hoax. There isn't such a place as Banjos and the story is clearly based on that of Woolpits. However, it surfaces from time to time in works on the paranormal and can lead the unwary astray.

Gervase of Tilbury, in the 13th Century, met a woman who actually claimed to have had a fairy encounter. The French believed the River Rhône to be tenanted by creatures called *dracs,* and Gervase tells us this woman was seized by a drac and forced to nurse his son. She couldn't see much under the water, but one day, when she was eating an eel pasty, she rubbed her eyes with some goo from it and thereafter could see clearly, despite her liqueous environment. Some time later, she was allowed to return home. One day she encountered the drac, who was surprised she could see him. He asked with which eye she could do this. When she told him, he touched the eye and she could see him no more. While this story seems to provide first hand evidence of a fairy encounter, here we have to proceed with caution. The same *motif* occurs elsewhere in folklore and we have to ask if this was the first time it occurred, giving rise over the centuries to other versions, whether similar encounters happened on a number of occasions, or whether Gervase or the woman simply made the whole thing up, perhaps using some local folktale as a source.

Gervase also mentions an incident which took place in Prussia at the monastery of Brunia. The monks had noticed, in the year 1138, that wine was disappearing from their cellar. They at length apprehended a dwarf down there, dark in complexion, who had been making his way in and out by a tunnel. They kept this creature in custody for a time, but it remained silent and refused all food. It quite startled a visiting bishop and made its escape. It was apparently seen no more.

There is a common fancy that very small fairies were not the object of belief until the Elizabethan era. However, turning to Gervase again, we find this is not the case. He speaks of tiny fairies called *portunes*. These were creatures wrinkled of face. They would visit houses and tidy them, and then cook themselves some frogs on the fire. Where Gervase obtained their name we do not know; perhaps it was from the Roman god *Portunus*, who presided over keys, doors and livestock. We do not find this name for diminutive beings mentioned again.

A Scotsman who was undoubtedly historical was Thomas the Rhymer, otherwise known as Thomas of Ercildoune, who throve in the 13th Century. You can still see the ruins of his family seat. He was the subject of a ballad which may be contemporary with him or nearly so. The Queen of Faerie took him to her husband's castle, where he stayed for a time. When she sent him home she gave him the gift of prophecy. On returning to the human realm, he found seven years had passed. It was said he eventually left home again, perhaps to return to Faerie. However, he seems to have been a religious man and it has been suggested that his absences were due to his going on retreat. Because poets were regarded as quasi-magical beings, his sojourn in Faerie may simply have been ascribed to him in popular lore.

Archbishop Burchard of Magdeburg (1295-1308) is said to have blessed the Holy Lake near Neuhoff in Germany, thus driving away water spirits that had much troubled the fishermen.

Shakespeare's *Romeo and Juliet* (?1590s) mentions for the first recorded time a fairy queen of diminutive stature named *Mab* and she is also mentioned by other poets. She is called the fairies' midwife. Whether Shakespeare took her from genuine folklore or just made her up is unknown. The suggestion that she is a variant of the Irish goddess *Maeve* ("intoxicatress") seems unlikely. This goddess seems to have first been associated with the hill of Tara (County Meath), later with Cruachan in the west of Ireland. She shares no characteristics with the Mab to whom Shakespeare refers.

In the 16th Century in Wales there supposedly existed a band of fairies known as *Gwylliaid Cochion*. This term has been translated as both the Red Fairies and the Red Bandits. They were supposed to have a single leader, they dwelt in the forest and did not build houses, and apparently engaged in depredations upon the local population. People absenting themselves from their homes would leave scythes in their chimneys to discourage ingress, but whether they did this because the iron would repel fairies or the scythes would prove dangerous to incoming bandits is not clear. The question that arises is, at the time, did the locals consider them merely bandits or raiding fairies, which was what folklore was later to make them? Sir John Wynn ab Meredydd and Baron Owain are said to have led an expedition against them in 1534, hanging some and exiling others. The *Gwylliaid* took bloody revenge, killing Owain, whose body was discovered with thirty arrows in it. Although many of the *Gwylliaid* were subsequently exiled, some of their descendants were said to be living in Llangarig as late as 1852. The whole story is somewhat dubious, the only certainty seeming to be that Owain's killing took place in 1552.

We might at this juncture mention Mr Hart, a schoolmaster. This worthy told John Aubrey, the antiquary, that one evening in 1633-4 he saw fairies dancing in circles. He was rooted to the spot, unable to leave. Then he tumbled to the ground and the fairies set upon him, pinching him all over. He was still there in the morning.

The Germans believed in a species called 'moss people'. These were supposed to be grey, aged-looking and the size of three-year-old children. One Hans Krepel is supposed to have encountered a moss woman in 1638 and conversed with her. A "female dwarf" was caught in Germany in 1644. A dwarf was seen near Dresden in the same year. A small being was seen a cellar in Lutzen in 1665. Yet another dwarf was seen in Torgau in 1669. This information comes from Janet Bord's book *Fairies* (1997), her source being Ulrich Magin, who is a well-known German investigator of anomalous phenomena.

While early historical accounts of encounters with the fairies verified by contemporary witnesses are not commonplace, accounts of the fairies themselves are certainly to be found. One who wrote what might even be dubbed a scientific account was a Scottish minister named Robert Kirk (1644-92). He reckoned fairies were a race between men and angels. This reminds us of a modern comment by the Jesuit writer, Herbert Thurston, who said that, while Christianity taught the existence of angels, men and demons, this did not preclude the existence of other races. Kirk was a graduate of the University of Edinburgh. He was a cleric of the Church of Scotland, a Presbyterian denomination. He studied beliefs in the fairies and garnered information from persons said to have the Second Sight (Gaelic: *An Da Shealladh*). These days this term is often used to mean those who can foretell the future, bur Kirk uses it to refer to those able to see the fairies, which may have been its original significance. He equates fairies with the *daemons* or nature spirits of the Ancient Greeks, referred to above. Their spirits (?souls) are intelligent. Their bodies, he avers, are like condensed clouds. They can appear and disappear at will. They take grain and may sometimes be heard baking bread. Their clothing tends to be the same as that of the country they inhabit. Their rulers are aristocratic and they have laws, but no religion. They have controversies, disputes and feuds.

Their houses are large and fair. They have lamps and fires which apparently run without fuel. Kirk avers there were women yet alive in his day who were taken by the fairies to nurse children. Once the children were weaned, they were allowed to go home or to stay with the fairies, or even killed. Kirk does not make it clear whether he actually spoke to these women. We must remember, however, that this was the era of Pastor Rahm in Sweden (*see* Introduction). Though Rahm's wife was taken to deliver, not nurse, a baby, we are here in an era that some interaction between human and fairy was not unheard of. Tales of women brought to deliver fairy babies are widespread.

The men with second sight (there are occasional women similarly endowed) go into "fits and raptures" to perceive the fairies. These sound somewhat like shamanistic trances. One man had been often seen to disappear and after about an hour become visible again. Kirk does not say whether he himself witnessed this.

A curious legend arose that, when Kirk died (or apparently died), he was taken into the fairy realm and a facsimile of his body left in his place. It is said that after his death he appeared to a doctor and told him to tell his cousin, a man named Duchray, that he would appear at the baptism of his posthumous daughter. If Duchray threw a knife over his head, Kirk would be retrieved. Kirk did appear at the baptism, but Duchray failed to throw the knife. Thus Kirk remains in Faerie.

On the Catholic side of things, the Franciscan theologian Ludovico Sinistrari (1622-1701) did not regard fairies as diabolical. They were, he opined, an animal species lower than the angels, but higher than humanity. He calls them demons, but is using the word in the sense of Greek *daemon*, which, as we have noted, could be applied to any kind of preternatural being. He calls the male of such a creature *incubus* and the female *succubus*. These terms were already in use for sex demons that seduced humans, but Sinistrari maintains they are solid, not spiritual, which seems to be a departure. He says that neither philosophy or theology is contradicted by the existence of beings such as he described. The offspring begotten of a union with an incubus or succubus was, in his day, of normal size. However, not all incubi/succubi were sexual predators or evil beings. They were capable of attaining salvation.

A curious tale is that of Anne Jeffries (1626-?1698). This woman had paranormal powers as a healer and claimed to have contact with the fairies. She was, in addition, a devout Christian.

When she was a servant girl (aged 19), she was knitting. She claimed that six diminutive men appeared and started kissing her, then bore her away to a fairyland, where she was the same height as everyone else. (Had she shrunk?) The land was one of temples and palaces, lakes full of gold and silver fish and many fragrant flowers. She herself was well attired. She favoured one of the six fairies who had brought her there and thereby excited jealousy. She was brought home. Such is the story as told by Hunt.[7] However, a contemporary London publisher, Moses Pitt, interested in the account, had it investigated and wrote a letter on the subject. Though the investigation seemed to confirm she had preternatural powers – one being the ability to appear and disappear at will – he makes no mention of her adventures in fairyland, merely stating that she had a fit, after which she was confined to bed and spent some time in recovering. Whether she was having some out-of-the-body experience during this time of illness is, of course, a subject for the paranormalist. Pitt's letter was dated 1699 and was consequently written near the time of the events. Anne ate fairy food, with which the fairies provided her, in preference to human food. A person to whom she gave some praised it highly.

Just what sort of experience Anne had is difficult to say. Her stay in Faerie may have been the result of feverish imagination which excited her preternatural powers. However, as she claimed continued contact with fairies who brought her food, we must suspect the presence of otherworldly beings here.[8] The fairy food delivered to her must have come from somewhere.

Strange beings, both humanoid and animal, were reported in the sky over The Hague in the Netherlands in 1645. Then a fleet of aerial ships, apparently crewed by humanoids, appeared. A battle took place between the two groups. Eventually, these aerial combatants seem to have disappeared, but a great cloud appeared in the sky.

---

7   Hunt, *Popular Romances of the West of England* (3rd ed.) First series.
8   K.I. Jones, *Anne Jeffries and the Fairies* (Penzance, 1996) contains most of Pitt's letter.

Another person to provide a story of the fairies that is allegedly based on fact is the bigoted anti-Catholic Richard Bovet, whose *Pandaemonium* appeared in 1684. He was told by a Captain Burton that, when the latter was in a tavern, he noticed a boy drumming with his fingers on the table. This occurred in Scotland. The boy told him that he regularly beat the drum for "a sort of people" at the hill between Edinburgh and Leith. When he came to the hill, a pair of gates would open for him. There were men and women within and many kinds of food and sometimes they would fly to France or Holland. Burton watched the boy, intending to follow him to the hill, but the boy eluded him.

Here we have a source that is quite near to actual contact with fairies. Of course, it is possible the boy was winding Burton up and it is also possible that Burton was winding Bovet up, but it is near enough to the fairies for us to consider it as hearsay evidence.

Bovet also tells us of a fairy market in Somerset, saying the incident had occurred about fifty years before. At a hill called Blackdown, not far from Taunton, a person riding home saw what was apparently a country fair. He rode towards it, having heard of the fairies there, and kept them in sight; but, when he arrived at the place, he could see no sign of them, but felt an invisible throng of people around him. He rode on and saw the market in the distance when he looked back. He developed a lameness in one side. Bovet says that others had also seen fairies in the area. Blackdown, by the way, is spelled *Blagdon* by Bovet. Ruth Tongue is supposed to have collected more modern tales of a fairy market in the vicinity, but she is a source that should be treated with caution.

This is the time when, according to the traditions of the Shangaan of South Africa, Queen Numbi lived. Suffering from an illness that might have been elephantiasis, she entered a star that had fallen to earth. Onlookers could discern small men in the star, from which the queen emerged rejuvenated and cured. Afterwards many animals in the area were born white, including an impressive elephant. This is merely a legend, but the interesting thing is that this is in the Timbavati region where white lions were born in modern times. Traditions in the area that such lions appeared from time to time had been scoffed at.

Another child with fairy connections was Johnny Williamson of Kirkudbrightshire who would disappear for days at a time, visiting his otherworldly friends. The words he used for the fairies were 'our folk' and on one occasion, when he had been missing for about ten days, he appeared beside some lunching peat-cutters and said he had emerged from a hole in the bog nearby.

Around 1750 a goblin-like creature, looking like a small oldster with very long hair, was said to be helping around a farm in Glaisdale (Yorkshire).

In Scotland a child named Jane Brown disappeared. A minister asked seven congregations to pray for her. In an hour she was found. She looked well-fed and her skin was slightly tinged with blue. It was generally believed she had been a pixy captive. [Tale recorded as true by James Hogg (1770-1835)].

In the 18th Century there were sightings of little men dancing around piles of gold and silver at Warton Crag (Lancashire).

An anonymous work, a little book written in verse, was entitled *Legends of the Moorlands and Forest in North Staffordshire* (1860). I understand the authoress was a Miss Darkeyene, whose name does not appear on the booklet. In this you will read that a few years before, the subterranean cavern coming out from Lud Church was inhabited by what is termed "a distinct race of beings".

The Reverend Sabine Baring-Gould was a prolific writer and scholar of the 19th Century. He writes that when he was four, he was being driven along on the box of a carriage by his father in France. Suddenly he saw hundreds of diminutive beings round about, about 2' tall, running beside their equipage. When he told his father, the latter put him inside the coach with his mother.

Baring-Gould's wife, when fifteen, saw a little man with beady black eyes, a foot to a foot-and-a-half tall. She was walking down a lane in Yorkshire and she saw him sitting on a hedge.

Baring-Gould's son, when collecting peapods, claimed to have seen a little man wearing a red cap, a green jacket and brown knee-breeches. His eyes were black and he had a grey beard.[9] Baring-Gould is inclined to assign these sightings to sunstroke, in his son's case augmented by images from *Grimms' Fairy Tales*.

Baring-Gould passed on to the folklorist Henderson the story of an encounter with a being called *The Radiant Boy*. It appears one John Mealyface was riding one night in Yorkshire when this entity, who appeared like an eleven-year-old boy with a shining face, rode past him on a white horse, which made no sound as it progressed. The Radiant Boy has also been associated with Lincolnshire.[10]

---

9   S. Baring-Gould, *A Book of Folklore* (Pulborough, 1993) cap. 9.
10 W. Henderson, *Notes on the Folk-lore of the Northern Counties of England and its Borders* (London, 1879) cap. VII.

A lady of Scottish origin told Henderson that there was a brownie in the peel house where she was born. When given clothes by the servants, the brownie left. This *motif* is familiar in folklore, i.e. helpful sprites leaving when given clothes.

An old woman named Elizabeth Cockburm told a Mr Surtees, who passed it on to Sir Walter Scott, that in 1744 two persons were hunting on the moors. The younger went to drink at a stream and a dwarf known as the Brown Man of the Muirs, of furious aspect, upbraided him for hunting the animals which were his subjects, but then invited the young man to his house. However, the latter was distracted by a shout from his companion and, when he turned back, the dwarf was gone.

In the 1850s, near the River Egray in Poitou, the small beings called *fadets* or *farfadets* in French folklore were reported pulling a strange vehicle with whining wheels. This is noted by the ufologist Jacques Vallee.

The village of Chimney Rock (population 175) in North Carolina seems to have had its fair share of preternatural beings. One report has it that in 1806 human figures were seen floating over the mountain, one of the witnesses being a Mrs Reaves.[11]

In 1811 two armies of horsemen were seen fighting in the air by mountaineers. These horsemen were also reported later.[12]

In 1891 a large number of bright beings were seen by many people on the side of the mountain.[13]

In 1855 a newspaper report, published four months after the alleged event, claimed a little man 18" tall was captured at Waldoboro (Maine).

James Gill in 1894 was on his way home from Wellington in Somerset when he saw what he described as a ring of fire. Beautifully dressed girls were dancing around a man with a yellow robe and crown who was singing. When Gill shouted and approached them, they disappeared.

The existence of some sort of portal in the area may be suspected, but it may also be that the onlooker could actually see through the portal into an otherworld of some kind.

Janet Bord who wrote the book *Fairies: Real Encounters with Little People* (1997) tells an interesting story set in 19th Century Ilkley Wells (Yorkshire) in 1815. William Butterfield, in charge of the baths here,

---

11 *Journal of Humanoid Studies*
12 *Journal of Humanoid Studies*
13 kitty the dreamerhubpages.com

was trying to get into the bath house one morning, but each time he tried to push open the door it was pushed back again. Butterfield gave one strenuous push and managed at last to open the door. Once in, he saw a crowd of little creatures in green, none above 18" high, apparently taking a bath with their clothes on. They began to leave and Butterfield called out "Hullo, there!" but this did not have the effect he had hoped, for the little creatures quitted the building expeditiously.

John Ireland (1879-1962), an English composer, had a strange experience at Harrow Hill in Sussex, locally said to be the last place fairies dwelt in England. I cannot trace the date of the experience, but he was having a picnic there when he found himself surrounded by what he took to be children, wearing clothes of a bygone era. They were almost silent, but were dancing. He looked away and when he looked back they were gone.[14]

In 1854 W. Crossing (1847-1928) saw a pixy at Sheeps Tor on Dartmoor. As he approached a cave pixies were said to inhabit, he saw one run out and suddenly disappear.

In 1855 a man in Maine claimed to have captured an 18" humanoid covered with black hair.

At some uncertain date in the 19th Century, children were digging at Piel Wyke (Cumbria) when they dug up a little cottage. It had vanished when they returned. Some days later, their father saw two diminutive beings on the hill, dressed in green. They disappeared into it.

Beyond the broad Atlantic in 1891, a man was woken in the night by the sound of music. He lived in El Dorado (Kansas). Gazing through his window, he saw diminutive beings, 18" tall, dancing. In due course, they disappeared.[15]

A 45cm tall man was spotted in the vicinity of Shaugh Bridge, Dartmoor, in 1897. The witness was a Mrs Herbert, then a child. She described the being she saw as a pixy.[16]

None of these accounts presents conclusive evidence. A sceptic could challenge any or all of them. However, due to the fact that a number involve alleged firsthand or near firsthand accounts, we cannot say that they are not evidence at all. We might call them *non-conclusive* evidence of the existence of fairies – indicators that fairies *might* exist. In this investigation, however, we are looking for probabilities rather than conclusive proof.

---

14 *Uncanny UK* (website)
15 Rife, p.82
16 *paranormaldatabase.com*

Chapter Three

the celts in the 19th century and afterwards

IT is surprising that there are so few witness-attested encounters with fairies from the Middle Ages. However, one must bear in mind that fewer people knew how to write then and any encounters were likely to involve illiterate country folk. By the time people came to write some of them down, they would probably be several generations old and no firsthand witnesses would have been to hand.

In the 19th and early 20th Centuries, however, folklore began to be perceived as a science. Peasants were questioned about their beliefs and some of those peasants claimed direct encounters with the fairy realm. At the same time, interest in Celtic materials started to flourish. One of the collectors was W.Y. Evans-Wentz (1878-1965), an American and a friend of Dr Douglas Hyde, who became the first President of Ireland. Hyde, though a sceptic himself, was a folklore collector and fluent speaker of the Irish language, which has not been completely displaced by English. Evans-Wentz also collected material in the other Celtic countries – Wales, Scotland, the Isle of Man, Cornwall and Brittany. W.B. Yeats (1865-1939) also collected a good deal of Irish material, reflected in his poetry and plays. The same is true of Lady Gregory (1852-1932), like Hyde a fluent Irish speaker. At perhaps a more scholarly level, Sir John Rhŷs (1840-1915) produced his monumental work on Manx and Welsh Celtic folklore. The Scottish nationalist Lewis Spence (1874-1955) produced a great deal of material, particularly from British and Irish sources.

In talking of Celtic parts, I should perhaps make clear where I mean and what the Celtic languages are:

Irish: a form of Gaelic spoken in Ireland.

Gaelic: a daughter language of Irish spoken in the Highlands of Scotland and parts of Canada. The term Gaelic is sometimes also applied to Irish, so to avoid confusion, I have called it Scottish Gaelic in this work.

Do not confuse it with *Scots*, the form of English spoken in Scotland, which was a separate language in the Middle Ages. There are still people who try to keep Scots as different from English as possible, such as by treating *porridge* as a plural noun. ("These porridge are lumpy.") This last fact is irrelevant, but I thought you'd like to know it anyway.

Manx: an offshoot of Irish spoken in the Isle of Man, now extinct. Because literacy died out there, a new form of writing was concocted, very different in orthography from Irish and Scottish Gaelic.

Welsh: a descendant of the language spoken by the ancient British. The ancient British language was once spoken all over England, but the Anglo-Saxon invasion displaced it. There is a Welsh-speaking community in Argentina.

Cornish: an extinct language, also descended from Ancient British, once spoken in Cornwall.

Breton: another descendent of Ancient British. It is spoken in Brittany, whither it was brought by British settlers about the 6th Century. The four main dialects are Gwenedeg, Kerneveg, Leoneg and Tregerieg.

In describing Manx and Cornish as extinct, I am aware of the efforts to revive them, so there are some speakers of each.

When describing fairy sightings listed by these writers, I shall stick to firsthand or at least secondhand reports. Reports from distant or attributed sources will as a rule be excluded.

In Ireland the fairies were not usually so called, a euphemism being used instead: *daoine maithe* (good people) in Irish and the Gentry (in English). We shall first look at witnesses interviewed by W.Y. Evans-Wentz, whose book on fairies was published in 1911. This book contains a number of accounts by witnesses or their acquaintances and I make no apology for using it extensively.

He writes of what he calls a seer, by which I take it he means a person known for his perhaps singular ability to interact with fairies. This seer is anonymous, but we learn he lived near Ben Bulben (County Sligo). When a young man, he and a friend encountered a male fairy dressed in blue, who warned him not to come to the area, as a young lady (a female fairy) wished to take him away. He also warned him against discharging his gun, as fairies didn't like noise.

On another occasion he met a fairy man who talked with him for some time, foretold his mother's death and told him to make sure she was given the last rites of the Church. He told him to get back into his house and that they (the fairies) could do nothing to him until he (the fairy) got back into the castle. The seer said he later discovered the fairy was going to abduct him, but changed his mind because he didn't want his mother to be left alone.

This is rather interesting. In advising that the mother be given Extreme Unction (now called the Sacrament of the Sick), the fairy showed no hostility to Christian rites. His decision not to abduct the seer shows a kindly disposition. Both of these things indicate a somewhat different attitude than is normally ascribed to fairies.

The seer told Evans-Wentz that the fairies are a military aristocratic race, far superior to humans. They have beautiful castles under the mountains. They are a distinct race from humans, occupying a status between humans and spirits. They have great powers and had said, "We could cut off half the human race, but would not, as we are expecting salvation." This would indicate some similarity to Christian belief, which some readers may find surprising.

The seer also said that, when they abduct a man, they can transmute his body to a body like their own. They are always young and death is unknown amongst them. If you eat their food when abducted, you cannot return to the place whence you came. They can appear in different forms. One who looked like a four foot dwarf said, "I am bigger than I appear to you now. We can make the old young, the big small and the small big." The seer differentiated between the Gentry and bad spirits and ghosts. Leprechauns, he averred, differed from the Gentry. He said his mother had once seen a leprechaun.

Ben Bulben, it may be noted here, is a site associated with Finn mac Cumhail, in origin a Celtic god named *Vindos* (the White One). He led a band of hunter gods called the *Fianna*.

A man named Michael Oates told Evans-Wentz that an acquaintance of his had once seen the Gentry hunting on the mountainside at night. They had horses and hounds. If these fairies were diminutive, it is difficult to see where they obtained their animals. They may have been of normal size. However, author Herbie Brennan and a companion, in 1971, spotted tiny horses at Longstone Rath (County Kildare). There were about 25 of them and none was larger than a cocker spaniel.

Pat Ruddy, a farmer, told Evans-Wentz that he hadn't been sure of the existence of the Gentry. Then, one night, he saw an army of them, clad in armour. He estimated their number at five or six thousand.

Mrs J. Conway of Rosses Point (also in County Sligo) said her husband had often seen the Gentry at night. They were the same size as humans.

Michael Reddy saw the Gentry on the strand at Lower Rosses Point. He first saw one of them who looked like an officer, pointing an object which might have been a sword at him. Later he saw a company of them, dressed in red, of human size.

If there is any truth in any of this, we can infer a number of possibilities – the fairies have shape changing abilities, great powers with which they could wipe out half of the human race, but must be in some way vulnerable themselves if they have to wear armour. The *motif* of the dangers of eating fairy food is widespread in folklore. Their bodies are different from humans, but they seem to be normally of human size. When the seer spoke of beautiful castles under the mountains, this sounds as though the mountains were a portal to another dimension, in which these castles existed. However, it must also be borne in mind that we know little about these informants. They had grown up in an atmosphere in which belief in the fairies was the norm. Some information about their psychology, whether they were subject to hallucinations, hysteria or any mental aberrations, would be very useful. Knowledge of instances of epilepsy or migraine amongst the witnesses would also be pertinent. However, the idea that some persons fall into a category called Fantasy Prone Persons, which has been put forward, should, on the basis of psychological investigation so far, be treated with caution.[17] The term has come into use since the 1980s and has become quite widespread.

A man called Ned Colton, who lived by Lough Derg (County Donegal) said that, when he was a boy, he and a number of others came within a few hundred feet of fairies dancing. A little woman struck his cousin across the face with what appeared to be a green rod. They ran home and the cousin apparently fell dead. A priest, Father Ryan, read psalms over her and struck her with his stole, reviving her.

A Mrs Megarry told Evans-Wentz that one night her father had been going for a doctor when, near Glenavy (County Antrim), he saw two regiments of Faerie coming towards him, one in red uniform, one in blue or green. They were playing music, but, when they parted to let him through the middle of them, they stopped playing until he had passed.

---

17 *Skeptic* website.

Lough Gur (County Limerick) was supposed to contain an entrance to Tír na nÓg, the land of the fairies. Every seven years the lake was supposed to dry up. Then a tree could be discerned, covered with a green cloth, and sitting beneath it a woman knitting. Countryfolk told Count John de Salis that they had seen what appeared to be fairy boat races on the lake, featuring four boats, each containing two men rowing and a woman steering. All seem to have been transparent.

A Kerryman who had been at Oxford with Evans-Wentz told him that in 1910, before Christmas, he and a companion had noticed a strange light, expanding and contracting. Then they noticed two lights. Each expanded into a yellow flame, about six feet high and four feet wide. In each was a radiant being. The lights joined and the beings started walking together. Both men had, before this, been of a sceptical outlook. The informant's brother, a doctor, who had hitherto also been a sceptic, later saw similar lights. Evans-Wentz' acquaintance said he saw phenomena like this again, both in Ireland and in England.

The reason I am citing these stories is to show that, if these people, who were claiming to be firsthand witnesses, had undergone delusions, delusions must have been frequent in County Sligo – and one must ask why. One must also allow for the possibility of mendacity, however – were these country folk simply telling Evans-Wentz, American tourist, what he wanted to hear? Not one of these stories is proof of fairies on its own, but the numbers of these stories indicate possible fact behind them.

About 1846, a fairy imbroglio was espied in the sky above Knockmaa (County Galway). This was at a time when Ireland's horrific Great Famine (Irish: *An Gort Mór*) was raging. Whether this might have engendered some form of hysteria leading to such assertions is an open question.

W.B. Yeats had a great interest in Irish myth and in an essay in *Bealtaine* published in 1900 said he had met four or five persons (sex unspecified) who claimed to have been the lovers of preternatural beings.

Evans-Wentz also took evidence in Scotland, going to the Isle of Barra (Gaelic: *Barraigh*) in the Outer Hebrides, where even today (2013) most are speakers of the Scottish Gaelic language. A John MacNeill on the island said his mother had once heard a fairy singing, while his father had said that fairies used to appear to people and vanish in front of them.

John Campbell, on the same island, told of his friend James Galbraith, who had been drinking at a fountain when he saw a woman dressed in green, whom he took to be a fairy. When he had finished drinking he walked away, but, looking behind, saw her vanish. His father, when told of the incident, said he too had seen the woman.

Campbell continued that his grandfather's neighbour, a widower, had married for the second time. The children of the second marriage were not well treated by the stepmother and a fairy, who had the appearance of an old man, gave one of them a splendid set of bagpipes and the skill to play them. The boy and his male descendants made outstanding pipers.

Some distinction seems to have been made on Barra between the *Sluagh* (preternatural host) and the fairies. The Sluagh were supposed to carry off men and ask them to shoot people. They would often shoot a horse or a cow instead. Marian MacLean told Evans-Wentz that her grandfather and father knew a man who had been carried by the Sluagh from the island of South Uist to Barra.

The Isle of Man is a British dependency (but not part of the United Kingdom) lying between Britain and Ireland. There Evans-Wentz was told by one Bill Clarke that he had seen a fleet of fairy boats. William Cain, better known as Willy-the-Fairy, claimed he often heard fairies singing and playing music. A Mr Leece told Evans-Wentz that a man named Keegan would disappear at night, for the fairies ("little men") would snatch him and use him as a horse.

A man called John Davies said he had been able to see fairies since he was eighteen or twenty. He said that, with the advance of education, people saw them less, but they were still there.

George Gelling of Ballasalla told Evans-Wentz that his apprentice claimed to have seen fairies dancing. He himself asserted he had heard fairy music. Rev. J.M. Spicer, the vicar of Mallow, was told by a lady that the fairies had tried to take her away. She had to call her son before they would stop. Canon Kewley said that, one evening, when driving along in a horse-drawn vehicle with his sister, he, she, their coachman and apparently their horse, saw a throng ahead of them, but, when they approached them, they melted away.

T.C. Kermode, MHK,[18] said he and a friend saw a crowd of little people, "no bigger than Tom Thumb". They were in a circle of light which Kermode referred to as "astral light". When his friend struck the

---

18 MHK = Member of the House of Keys, lower house of the Tynwald (Manx Parliament). The House of Keys (Manx, *Kiare as Feed*) dates from at least 1417.

road with a stick and shouted, they vanished. Kermode said old people in Man claimed to have seen fairies hunting with hounds and horses and on the sea in ships.

Although Evans-Wentz produces much Welsh fairy lore, he is rather short on actual encounters. He does tell us the story of Mrs Catherine Jones, from whom he heard it at first hand. She informed him that she had once encountered a good-looking lady of normal human size. She tried repeatedly to touch her, but her hand always went through her. When she asked the lady why she did not speak, she disappeared.

The section on Brittany in Evans-Wentz' book features an introduction by Anatole Le Braz (University of Rennes). He spoke of an apparition called Groac'h Lanascol, who was supposed to occupy a ruined château. Many claimed to have seen her, but there were varying descriptions. Some said she was an old woman with crutches, who stirred the dead leaves, turning them into gold. Some said she looked like a richly adorned young princess attended by little black men. When she stopped in front of a tree, it would bow down, as though to receive orders. If she looked at the water of a pool, it would tremble.

Evans-Wentz mentioned the name *Vivian* to an old woman. This is the name of Merlin's innamorata in Arthurian romance and, as Arthurian legends are known in Brittany, the same person may be intended. The woman said her husband, who had been poaching, had been surprised by keepers, who shot him in the leg. He was about to let himself be killed rather than surrender when a thick mist surrounded him and a voice said to save himself, the spirit of Vivian would watch over him until he had crawled out of the forest. This happened in the Forest of Brocéliande, which was known for its fairy reputation. The forest is now called Paimpont.

In rural Brittany there is a small lake called the Mirror of Fairies. The Seven Fairies of Koncorret were said to have lived nearby, hiding during the day, emerging during the night. One of them fell in love with a man and fought with the others. They reddened the valley with their blood.

Although I have cited evidence from Evans-Wentz at some length, I trust it has been worthwhile to do so. However, he is, of course, not the only source for 19th Century Celtic sightings. Fairies were reported at Beddgelert (Gwynedd) in the 19th Century. Elizabeth Andrews, writing of Ulster folklore, mentioned a sighting in the Mourne Mountains (County Down) of little beings with red hair. The night was stormy. In the same county, a woman at Tullamore Park saw beings with scanty clothing. Their hair stood up like horses'. This sounds a little like a Mohican hairstyle.

An interesting account appears in a 19th Century Irish periodical.[19] A boy disappeared from his home and a changeling was left in his place. The priest was called in. He managed to recall the boy, but only for a few minutes, and the boy told him how he might be retrieved. Then he was replaced once more by the changeling.

The priest took the changeling to Lough Lane (County Westmeath) into which he dipped it three times. The boy emerged and walked across the water to his father. They set off for home, escorted by a line of soldiers which had emerged from the lake. The boy's mother was instructed to keep silent. However, she spoke. The boy had to return to the lake and, when they returned home, the changeling was once again there. Picking the changeling up, the priest returned to the lake and repeated the procedure. This time the boy was returned for good.

This episode is dated 1860, nearly thirty years before the article was written, but the narrator seems sincere in describing it and it would appear it contains at least a nucleus of truth.

In 1866 in Ballygown (Ireland) the occupants of a house suffered from a plague of objects being thrown at their windows. The Little People were blamed.

The Welsh periodical *Bye-Gones* contains a couple of interesting Welsh encounters. The first was told to the narrator by C.T., for whose veracity the narrator vouches. He was travelling over Bedwellty Mountain. Suddenly, he found fairies all around him and heard the sound of a hunting horn. He had been told that, if he drew his knife, any fairies seeing him would vanish. He did this and the fairies disappeared.[20]

A man named Robert Jones, who lived 'in former days' in Wales was woken by little people dancing in his room and a little fiddler playing with zest. The fiddler, who seemed a merry soul, told him they were spirits of the air. He said they were coming back again on the following day, but Jones threatened to tell the landlord.[21]

In the first case we see the belief that iron wards off fairies. This was formerly used as an argument to show that iron-wielding invaders had defeated a copper-wielding native race.

---

19 *Irish Fireside,* 7th January, 1884.
20 *Bye-Gones,* May 13th, 1885.
21 *Bye-Gones,* January 4th, 1899.

Staying in Wales, the BBC interviewed a number of ladies who, about fifty years before – about 1907 – had had an experience with fairies. At Kingsheriot Farm in Pembrokeshire they saw some little men wearing green knee breeches. Their shoes were turned up at the toes. Their hands looked like claws and had only four fingers. They seemed to be playing on a harvesting binder. The girls fled. Later certain Romanies said the knew all about the little people, who lived in nearby woods.[22]

In Ireland, fairy expert and seanchaí (traditional storyteller) Eddie Lenihen obtained the following story in 1975 from a man in his late 70s. The events, which the narrator averred were true, had befallen his grandfather. His grandfather was building a house when a passing man advised him not to build it in that spot. The grandfather ignored him and he and his wife moved into the house when it was completed. They got no sleep, however, due to crashing noises coming from downstairs every night, though no damage was done. Meeting the passing man again, the grandfather asked him the reason for the noise. He was told that he had built his house between two whitethorns, which showed it was on a fairy path. The remedy was to make another door in the back wall, which had been impeding the fairies' progress along the path. This the grandfather did and the sleepless nights came to an end. However, once every year those in the house would wake up and smell cooking. Three days later, one of their cattle would die. The narrator told this to Lenihen in the house and he pointed out that the doors were never locked at night, because they were always found open in the morning. Lenihen saw the doors.[23]

Let us return, if we may, to the Isle of Man. Here George Waldron, in the 18th Century, waxed wroth at the hegemony of the clergy.[24] But he added that the people probably had an even greater reverence for the fairies. He was told by a woman who used to serve him with butter that her daughter, when sent on an errand, was stopped on a mountain top by little people. Some urged her to go with them, but one defended her and said they should not take her, so they beat her and let her go.

Waldron has other surprising stories from Man. An educated man told him he had never believed in fairies until one day he approached a group of what he took to be schoolboys, but they vanished before his eyes.

22 J. Bord *Fairy Sites* (Glastonbury, 2004) p.180
23 E. Lenihen *Meeting the Other Crowd* (Dublin, 2003) pp.149-61.
24 G. Waldron *The History and Description of the Isle of Man* (London, 1744) p.62

Another man, whose veracity Waldron respected, told him that he had been on his way to sell a horse. A little man in plain dress asked to buy the horse and offered him seven pounds. The deal being completed, the little man climbed onto the horse. Both rider and steed vanished into the ground, leaving Waldron's informant "in the utmost terror and consternation".

An Englishman, a friend of Waldron, when crossing a river on horseback, heard a wonderful symphony, which he took to be fairy music.

Waldron has an interesting story about a mermaid city, which we shall relate when we come to deal with those beings.

A look at some further Welsh cases will not, I trust, go amiss. In July 1760, a number of persons at Bedwellty (the name of a constituency abolished in 1983) saw a large flock of sheep apparently disappear. Then they came back, but the onlookers saw that they were in differing forms – as hounds, pigs or infants. The witnesses were described as "credible".[25]

The author of the book from which the previous story was taken, one E. Jones, had a relation referred to only by the initials E.T. He was travelling over the Bedwellty Mountains when he saw fairies and heard a bugle winded. He drew his knife, which he had been told was a protection against fairies, presumably because it was made of iron, and they vanished. This may be the same incident related in *Bye-Gones*.

The same book (pp. 33-4) speaks of Rees John Rosser. One morning, when in a barn, he lay on some hay to rest. He heard music outside, then a company of people in striped clothes entered and proceeded to dance. One of them, a woman, placed a cushion with tassels under Rosser's head. When the cock crew, they left, taking the cushion with them.

Mr Jones supplies us with other stories. In the parish of Bessaleg one Anne William Frances saw a company of fairies dancing. She brought them a pail of water. The next time she went there they gave her a shilling. This practice continued until she told her mother (p.43).

In 1884 two Welsh miners in Virginia City (Nevada) saw two hammers being worked by invisible labourers in an American mine. They probably ascribed the activity to mine fairies, called *knockers* in Britain and *tommyknockers* in the United States.

---

25 E. Jones *A Relation of Apparitions of Spirits in the County of Monmouthshire and the Principality of Wales* (Newport, Monmouthshire, 1813) pp. 23-24

Dermot MacManus wrote *The Middle Kingdom*, a work on Irish fairies, in 1959. The American edition was entitled *Irish Earth Folk*. The encounters described below are undated, but are probably from the 20th Century rather than the 19th. However, they are in the tradition of the Celtic accounts given above and they occur in Ireland.

Nora, the niece of a Colonel Jordan, was dressing for dinner, when a child in the room told her there was a man there. Nora saw him. He was about four feet tall, wore a green hat with no brim, a yellow waistcoat and a cravat. He had knee-breeches and grey socks. He had no beard. Then he vanished in front of her.

The man appeared again at dinner, when Nora drew the Colonel's attention to him. The Colonel saw him briefly.

An old retainer called Michael told the Colonel he had seen him at the front of the house when he was eighteen. The little man vanished before his eyes. When he told others, a maid said she had seen the little man often. MacManus' informant was the Colonel himself.[26]

Another sighting was near Cranagh, near Borris-in-Ossory (County Carlow). A girl of about nine was bringing in cows when she saw a fairy man, who looked at her in friendly fashion and crossed a ditch, disappearing into the solid earth of the bank. When the girl grew up, she became a nurse and was MacManus' informant.[27]

At Foxford (County Mayo) two boys aged nine and ten encountered what appeared to be a leprechaun. He had been hiding from them behind a stone. He had a black coat which seemed to be made of a rich material, perhaps silk or satin. His face was broad and somewhat flat. He had a sort of beard which ran around his chin from one ear to the other. He gave the boys a friendly grin, but they ran away. When one of the boys grew up, he became a doctor and he was MacManus' informant.[28]

The website Skygaze informs us that in the early 20th Century, Mari Sion of Llanddeusant on the island of Anglesey in Wales was at home with her family one night when they heard a knocking at the door. Outside were a little man, woman and baby. The little woman asked Mari to leave a bowl of water and a coal of fire so she could wash the baby when the family went to bed. This Mari did and during the night the family heard sounds of activity. Next day, the family found the house tidy, but the bowl upturned. Under it they found

---

26 D. MacManus *The Middle Kingdom* (London, 1959), cap. II
27 *Ibid.*
28 *Ibid.*

four shillings (20p). Mari is said to have told this personally to a folklorist, who is not named.

Appendix

Lady Gregory's Researches

Lady Gregory (1852-1932) did a great deal of research in Irish folklore and unearthed many stories of Irish fairies, including allegedly true ones. Her Visions and Beliefs in the West of Ireland *was published in 1920, but, as the events in the accounts are undated, they may have occurred a considerable time before.*

A boy living in Dunraven, known to Lady Gregory's informant, had a settle bed in the kitchen and awoke one night to find the room full of fairies.

A man from County Clare told Lady Gregory that he had seen a field full of fairies riding about on horses. He compared them to jockeys. They were little people and one supposes the horses were of proportionate size. (*For accounts of similar small horses, see below.*) They had set up a jump made of bushes and urged the horses to leap over it. The Clare man's companions didn't see the fairies, but heard their horses.

J. Creevy was told by a man named Lee that he had seen "red men" riding through the country and going over ditches. By this, hedges may have been meant, as in Hiberno-English *ditch* is used to mean *hedge*, a confusion that possibly arose when the Irish began to speak English.

J. Fagan left a party at two o'clock and was walking through the night when he saw a small woman, 3' in height. She wore a white cap with a frilled border, a red "square" (? upper garment) and a red petticoat. Fearing the Little People, Mr Fagan began to run, but she pursued him back to his house.

Mrs Cloonan, when milking a cow, saw two little men. She did not make out their faces. She became distracted by the cow and when she looked back they were gone.

Simon Niland told Lady Gregory he knew a number of people who had seen the fairies.

Mrs Hynes told Lady Gregory that her neighbour was coming home when he beheld a big man climbing over the wall. The big man grew bigger and bigger. Her informant nearly fainted.

An islander (we are not told from which island) told Lady Gregory that one night when he was coming home, his dog seemed to have a fight with an invisible entity.

John Madden said that his sister-in-law had seen a group of them playing hurling, wearing red caps and blue. They saw a throng of them looking on. By "them" the fairies are meant.

Old Doran said he saw a fairy fair near Castle Hacket. This he told Peter Heffernan, who passed it on to Lady Gregory. Heffernan said his wife encountered a little man whom she disturbed one day on her way to Mass.

John Phelan cutting trees in Inchy one day saw a tall girl picking nuts. Her hair hung over her shoulders. Her head was uncovered. Her dress was simple. When she saw Phelan approaching, she vanished.

Lady Gregory was informed by an Aran man – she does not tell us if he came from the Aran Islands in County Galway or Aran Island in County Donegal – that, when he was setting out manure in his garden, the fairies came, rolled it up, tossed it over the wall and carried it out to sea.

A friend of Thomas Brown's crossing a field saw many fairies, among them people he knew to be dead. Their talk was like the hissing of geese. There was a big man apparently in charge and his voice sounded like the rolling of a barrel.

A spinning woman told Lady Gregory she once saw a leprechaun. He was wearing a red jacket. When he saw her, he fled.

Mrs Barrett said her husband woke up one night and, it being bright, he went outside and saw a fairy hurling match in progress.

Mrs Barrett also said that one Micky Smith had seen the fairies in the air above Cahir.

Mrs Casey spoke of Kate Cloran, her friend, and she claimed a throng of fairies had led her astray on one occasion. They wore white blouses and black skirts and some wore crimson mantles. They had golden hair and were very beautiful.

A man who lived by the sea spoke of the experience of his father. He saw about twelve ladies in white dancing in a circle and a musician in the middle.

A man named Callan told Lady Gregory that Father Hobbs, a priest, had seen a large number of them.

Chapter Four
LittLe peopLe (aNd otheRs)

WE now come to encounters with fairies in modern times, by which I mean 1900 or subsequently. When you reach my age, "modern" goes a long way back. I have divided the fairies into categories, and the accounts, unless the contrary is stated, are supposed to be true. I say *supposed* because it is well outside the ability of many a reader to believe that fairies might exist outside the human imagination. Moreover, I myself was not present at the events they describe. However, read what is here and believe what you will.

In saying the above, I do not discount the possibility of misperception, hallucination or sheer mendacity where these accounts are concerned. I have not excluded experiences that the narrator has learned from a friend, but I have tended to be chary of anything passed on from a friend of a friend. Such stories these days are referred to as *foaflore* and are treated with consummate caution.

Because of the number of sightings, I intend to give them in yearly order. The following abbreviations are used for sources, full details of the written ones being given in the Bibliography.

CF	A. Conan Doyle *The Coming of the Fairies*
F	Janet Bord *Fairies*
FG	Fairy Gardens (website)
FS	Janet Bord *Fairy Sightings*
FT	*Fortean Times* (periodical)
FTL	K.M. Briggs *The Fairies in Tradition and Literature*
GP	P. Narvaez (ed.) *The Good People*
JHS	Journal of Humanoid Studies (website)
I	B.M. Nunnelly *The Inhumanoids*
LP	Ron Quinn *Little People*
MacManus	D. MacManus *The Middle Kingdom* (aka *Irish Earth Folk*)
NEO	New England Oddities (website)
PAC	Paranormal About.com (website); also About.com – Paranormal

PND   Paranormal Database (website)
Rife   Rife *America's Nightmare Monsters*
SFP   J. Dathen *Somerset Fairies and Pixies*
Steiger B. Steiger *Out of the Dark*
Varner   G.R. Varner *Folklore of Faeries &c.*
WL   K. Mullin *The Wondrous Land*

1904

Brian, an employee of Dermot MacManus' grandmother, heard music and dancing coming from a garden house where he was working. Laughter and talking were also audible. When he approached the house, the sounds ceased. He looked inside and it was empty. There was a fairy hill nearby. When he had left the house, he heard the music and dancing break out again.

1909

A Maine newspaper identified a humanoid which had been seen in this year as the *New Jersey Gargoyle*.

1910

The next case I mention is taken from Albert Rosales' outstanding website, the *Journal of Humanoid Studies*. The creatures described may not, in fact, be of the fairy kind at all, but what they were is something of a mystery. In Guyana (then known as British Guiana) in 1910 a resident magistrate saw diminutive humanoids covered in reddish-brown fur. As he watched, they made their way into the jungle, never taking their eyes off their observer. These unidentified creatures are unlikely to have been monkeys, as I feel the witness would have made reference to their tails. There are no apes in South America known to modern zoology, but this doesn't mean they aren't there. There is still quite a lot of forest down there in which they might hide. There is, moreover, a legendary creature called the *didi*, which corresponds closely with the creatures described. This is supposed to be found in both Guyana and French Guiana. As Suriname is between the two, one should possibly look for them there as well. However, the term didi is also applied to larger hominids rumoured to dwell in the area. [JHS]

The next encounter comes from a friend of a friend tale, so I treat it with appropriate caution. The year in which it is supposed to have occurred was about, but not certainly in, 1910. It was told by a church elder to the Reverend Alexander Fraser and allegedly took place on the Scottish island of Muck. Two fairies, equally fluent in English and Gaelic, appeared to a couple of boys, whom they quizzed about their home. A tiny woman in a little boat, with a dog the size of a rat, was offshore. They were offered and ate tiny loaves of bread. The fairies told them they would not be coming back, but others of their race would come. [F]

A woman only identified as Mrs H wrote to Conan Doyle, saying she had once seen a fairy. (The year is approximate.) It was in the long grass and flowers in a wood in West Sussex and it was about 6" tall.

1911

In the Arctic wilds of North America an exploratory party led by Captain Yvolnoff found small human footprints. These led to a hole. They put a dog into it, but it came out pretty quickly. A diminutive humanoid emerged from the hole in due course. Others followed. Their language was incomprehensible and their Eskimo guides had never seen their like. In all, they totalled four families of 27 people. They seemed to lack knowledge of fire and had only their clothing to protect them from the rigours of the climate. There was a kind of fish resembling a trout readily available and these they would pick up in their hands and eat raw.

The first man to emerge was about 3'-4.5' tall with a head that almost bore the shape of a triangle. There was a tuft of hair on the top of his head. The beings had high voices. [E. Ferrill, *Strange Stories of Alaska and the Yukon*]

1914

At a wood in the vicinity of Santiago del Estero, Argentina, a female diminutive person in green shiny clothing chased a girl in the woods. She or another similar being was seen by another girl. [JHS]

Two diminutive beings were reported by two boys in Caerphilly (Wales). The boys' surnames were Uden and Hopkins. The beings, wearing tall hats, had glowing eyes. [I]

1917

This is the year when the famous Cottingley Fairy Photographs, which successfully fooled Conan Doyle, came to light. There is some doubt that one of these fairy photographs is really a hoax. However, the girls who took them said they had actually seen fairies and had faked the photographs to make people believe them. Frances Griffiths, one of the girls, maintained that one of the photographs was genuine. People still turn up at Cottingley in Yorkshire looking for the fairies.

1918

This is the year that Pamela Frankau underwent the fairy experience described by her in the Introduction.

1919

Harry Anderson (13) one night near Barron (Wisconsin) saw a troop of twenty little men. They were white-skinned and bald, wearing knee pants and braces. They passed him by, paying no attention to him. They made mumbling sounds. [skygaze.com]

1920s

W.S. Jones, a schoolboy of 8 or 9, saw a 3' tall old-looking man wearing a red cap and dressed in green from the waist down. This happened at Llanystumdwy (Gwynedd). [F]

Reports of *kakamoras* in the Solomon Islands were made in this year. These creatures are diminutive beings on Guadalcanal and San Cristoval.

1921

A driver on a country road saw a little man about 18" tall. He had a pointed cap. [naturalplane.blogspot.com]

1927

Paul Starzman of Indiana, hiking in a gravel pit, came on a little man 2' high or less. He had thick blond hair. His face was round and pinkish.

He wore a light blue gown and was barefoot. Starzman and a friend saw another one later. He identified the being as one of the *Pai-i-sa-ki*, the Little People of Miami Indian legend. [Steiger]

1929

The *Flying Saucer Review* reported that in this year two children, aged five and eight, saw a tiny man, wearing a tiny flying helmet in a tiny flying machine, which landed briefly. It then took off. [F]

Bud Landis [pseudonym] was walking home one night when he noticed a strange light in the woods nearby. He went to investigate. He saw a light the shape of a dome. It was roughly 4' high and 18" wide. When the light became brighter, Bud hid. Out of the light stepped two little men, each about 1' tall. Bud leaped back and the little men went back into the light, which vanished. This happened in the Catskills in New York state. [LP]

1930

A small man, 4'3" tall, ran out of a ditch and glided, without using his legs, across the road, startling a French motorist at Toul-St-Croix. [JHS]

A man in Wayne County (Tennessee) was pursued by little men on Beech Court Road, eventually fainting. [JHS]

1930s

A couple named David and Betty lived at Hurleyville (NY). One night when they were out walking they saw a little man hanging from the branch of a tree. David later found a knothole in the tree which he thought was the little man's home. They saw him again in spring and he smiled in friendly fashion. [LP]

At Worlebury, an ancient British earthwork, a fairy or pixy was seen briefly in a coppice. [Codd *Mysterious Somerset and Bristol*]

1933

John (surname withheld) aged 10 saw, in the Catskills in New York state, a bird which he could not identify carrying a little man on its back. [LP]

1935

A witness (aged 13) saw a little woman, clad in red, about 2' tall, in County Donegal, Ireland. The witness fled. [JHS]

1938

The Dublin *Irish Press* (now defunct) told this story of John Keeley of County Limerick, a schoolboy. He encountered a fairy. He told his friends, who suggested he talk to it. Keeley did so and asked the little being where he came from, to which he received the reply, "I'm from the mountains and it's all equal to you what my business is." Next day John saw two little men and held the hand of one. His friends were in the bushes, watching all this. The little men twigged what was going on and ran off, pursued by Keeley and his associates. They ran through hedge, ditch and bog, but the little men remained clean while Keeley had his friends were presumably not so fortunate. The height of the little men was about 2', their faces were hard and hairy, they lacked ears, they wore red clothing and knee-breeches, one having a white cape. Needless to say, Keeley and Co did not catch up with them. [F]

Friends of Dermot MacManus named Coleman had stopped their caravan for an overnight rest. A woman suggested to Mrs Coleman that she leave butter out for the fairies. Mrs Coleman paid no heed, but later decided she would leave butter out underneath the caravan as it was cool there. She placed an inverted plate over it and put a stone on top of that. The bowl was in the same state next morning, but when she took off the plate she found two-thirds of it gone. Half had been sliced out, as though with a knife. Of the remainder, half had been scooped out. No animal could have done this and if a human were to blame, why would he go to so much trouble to replace the bowl as he found it? The butter had been positioned under a compartment of the caravan containing two dogs.

1939

Fairy music was heard by schoolchildren at Bridport (Dorset) on Colner's Hill. It had been heard on previous occasions. [PND]

Mike Dunlop, a teenager, was in the woods of New York state near the Delaware River. He came on some rocks and was astonished to discover a little door in them, complete with doorknob and hinges. He tried the door, but it was locked. He then hid amongst the trees and, after a long wait, the door opened and a little face looked out. It was that of a small man with a beard and hat. Then the door slammed shut. When he later returned to the rock with his father, the door was not there. [LP]

1940 approx./1940s

The reason this date is approximate is because the witness only stated that it happened during World War II. The location is the island of Hoy, in the Orkney Islands, off the north coast of Scotland. The Orkney population is largely of Norse origin and the name they use for Little People there is *trows*. These are sometimes maritime. W.E.Thorner, during the War, saw little wild men with long hair and sallow faces dancing in a storm on Torness, where they seemed to fling themselves over a cliff. [F]

There was also a sighting of fairies in the 1940s on a track leading from Chidcock to Langdon Hill in Dorset. [FS]

In the 1940s Jill, a little girl, wandered too far from her aunt's home in the Catskill Mountains and became lost in the woods. She met with two little people whom she described as dolls and asked for directions. They indicated that she should follow them. When darkness fell, balls of light appeared around the diminutive beings. Then all three speeded up, like a film being fast forwarded. They reached the aunt's house. Jill turned to thank her rescuers, but they had vanished. [LP]

Over forty children and their teacher in Hawaii claimed to have seen *menehune*, the diminutive beings of Hawaiian folklore. These little people may represent an early race of invaders in the islands. In 1820 King Kaumualii of Kauai (died 1824) conducted a census of his kingdom, which listed 65 people as menehune. They seem to have been known and recognised then. It has also been contended, however, that the idea of little people was brought to the islands by Europeans. It is possible that this is so and that later folklore gave the menehune a small stature that they did not originally possess.

1942

Ron Quinn (born 1932) was a small boy who went on holiday to Mongaup Valley (NY), where his father and mother had rented a cabin.

One day Ron was alone in the cabin when he heard tapping on the window. Outside he saw a little man, tapping and waving. He had a grey beard, silky hair extending to his shoulders, a grey shirt, short trousers and grey boots.

Ron opened the window, but the little man stepped backwards before he could be touched. Then he jumped down and ran off across the grass.

Ron's story appeared in a paper in 1989 and he asked readers for accounts of experiences of the same kind as his own. He was flooded with letters, out of which he made a fascinating book on the subject. [LP]

1947

A Russian countrywoman approached some men sitting at a fire in the forest. When she came close, she saw they were dwarfs with greenish faces. They fled on her arrival. [JHS]

1948

When at night in the woods near Horsham (Sussex), E.J.A. Reynolds (10) saw a little man only 18" tall. His face looked leathery, but he appears to have been beardless. He had a long nose. Reynolds claimed he had seen the man on a later occasion from the upper deck of a bus. [F]

S.B. Shembel (aged 13) in Moscow saw a humanoid in his bedroom when he awoke. Its body was covered with dark hair and it seemed two dimensional. [JHS]

Just south of Mongaup Valley (NY) one of Anna Pratt's aunts was about to set off in her car with her son. The son (aged 6) didn't want to leave, saying he wanted to play with "the little man". His mother went to see who this was and was astonished to discover a small man about 2.5' tall. He seemed to be trying to warn her about something. She had a car accident on her way home that night. [LP]

1949

Mr Hobson of New York state found little men taking eggs from his hen house. [LP]

1950

Mrs Ellen Jonerson saw a tiny person, at most a foot in height and of stocky build. She summoned her friend and the pair saw him waddle away. [JHS]

1951

Two sisters saw a little man in Wicklow, Ireland. He was dressed in black and wore a black cap but was not old. They grew frightened and ran through a gateway into a field, closing the gate behind them. The little man watched them. They looked back later and found the little man had disappeared. [MacManus, cap. 2]

1952

Mrs C. Woods, walking on Dartmoor, saw a little man in a brown smock, tied about the waist. His leggings were also brown. When she drew nearer, he retreated behind a boulder. When she looked behind the boulder, she could find no trace of him.

At Lake June (California) J.Peterson saw a kind of cone which seemed to have burrowed its way out of the earth. A little man exited it. Then he returned to it and it went down into the earth once more. [JHS]

Two young men were riding along in New Mexico when they encountered a little man covered in spots. They rode past him, only to discover he was on the horse behind one of them. [Varner]

1954

A glowing-eyed diminutive being was reported from Algeria on October 24th. [I]

A walking being resembling a sugar cube was seen by children at Premanon (Franche-Comté). It gave them an electric shock. It left in a fireball which left a flattened fairy ring on the ground. [magonia.haan. com]

1955

R.D. Jameson, a folklorist, recorded an encounter in the United States in this year. His informant's grandmother and her sister were sleeping in a forest overnight. They awoke and discovered a group of little men, who made a ring of apples and then played around them. This occurred in New Mexico.

The Eastman family were picnicking in the Catskills. Some of the fruit went missing and young Tim, looking for his ball that had gone out of sight, parted some grass to find a little man holding the fruit. Tim had only a moment to see him before he dashed off. The little man had no beard, his feet seemed too big and he had a pack on his back. His clothing seemed strange. Tim's brother and possibly his sister also saw the little man. [LP]

1956

Some persons at a campfire in Shark Bay, Australia, saw an old man with shrivelled skin. He seemed able to communicate with two members of the party. A witness said they turned up from time to time to trade for sugar and flour. [Shuker, p.30]

1957

A witness claimed to have seen two little people with very little hair and unusual, shabby clothes near Fort Worth (Texas). However, he admitted he had been asleep and was still sleepy. [PAC]

1959

On swampy ground at Charles Mill Lake (Ohio), a humanoid, 7' in height and luminous, was discerned by three witnesses. As far as they could see, it did not have any arms. The eyes were large and greenish. [JHS]

1960s

Joe and Linda [surname withheld] were driving through the Catskills in New York state at night when they heard a thud on the roof of their car. They heard several further sounds. Joe stopped the car and got out, bearing his trusty flashlight, to discover a terrified little man who had been clinging to the roof. He jumped off and ran. [LP]

1964

The Ribble, a river near Preston (Lancashire), was the site of fairy sightings. Little green men, 3" tall, were seen by a doctor. They were walking in Indian file along the bank of a river. Tiny figures were seen by other witnesses climbing a tree in nearby Penwortham Woods. [FS]

On June 30th, children in Liverpool reported a number of little men in Jubilee Park. They wore white hats and threw sods at each other. Some people said they were *leprechauns,* an identification perhaps arising from the large number of people of Irish ancestry in Liverpool. [*Beachcomber website*]

1965 (approx.)

A female student in Muncie (Indiana) noticed that two little men, each about 2' tall and clad in tree bark garments, were watching her. [Rife: 85]

1967

At Arc-sous-Cicon in France on July 17th a girl reported seeing some diminutive beings whom she labelled *Chinese.* A number of other children went to investigate and saw a little being, about 3' tall, running faster than was possible for a human. He was somewhat abdominals. He ran into a bush. A voice was heard. The scared children ran off.

1968

George Grey of Kempsey, Australia, was set upon by a hairy dwarf like create as he slept in a bush hut. Its eyes looked like those of a human, its nose was large and the face, which was hairless, was the colour of copper. [Smith, *Bunyips and Bigfoots*, p.164]

1969

A 19-year-old American woman, whose husband was serving in Vietnam, was visited in the night by what she called a gnome. He had entered through the open window. He sat on the end of her bed, smoking a pipe. She could see through him. He told her that her husband was in trouble, but would be all right. When he left, she called in her mother, who was in the same house. Her mother noticed the smell of smoke.

Next day the Army called to let her know her husband had been injured, but would be all right and would be home soon. [natural plane.blogspot.com]

1970s

In a house in Mary Tavy (Devon), two brothers shared a bedroom. One was astonished to see little lights enter the room and dance around. They then changed into little people, colourfully dressed. [PND]

A motorist in Australia saw small, naked, dark people running across the road between Port Holland and Broome (Western Australia). [Shuker, p. 30]

A 5-year old girl in Wandsworth, London, saw a diminutive being in the fireplace. He was dressed in green with a red hat. She went to lift him up, but he smiled and vanished. [Arnold *Mystery Animals of the British Isles: London*]

1971

John Stephan (9) woke up to see under his window an "elf or gnome" with hat and beard. He estimated its height at 2'. It moved strangely, as though gravity did not affect it very much. [About.com – Your True Tales, April 2006]

1973

Two tiny girls and a boy were spotted near Liberty (NY) by Mike and Sally Ellsworth. [LP]

Walking along near the banks of the Mongaup River (NY), Peter Winters saw a little man fishing. He wore a hat, had light brown clothing and was bearded. He was about 2' tall. [LP]

1974

A summer worker, who later became a doctor, was on his way to St Louis (Missouri) by bus. Looking across the aisle he saw a girl who looked like an elf. She appeared to be enveloped in a greenish light. He closed his eyes. When he opened them, she was gone. [PAC]

Birdwatcher Jim McGill was in the wood near Liberty (NY), when he heard the sound of voices. He discovered two small men, who hadn't noticed him, talking in a foreign tongue. They were clad in green, wore wrinkled caps and had beards. A third being joined them and they eventually departed. [LP]

1975

In July, school pupils of Australia saw 8 hairy dwarfs about 2' tall with white glaring eyes. It is probable that they were *junjudees*, creatures of Aboriginal folklore. [*Sun Herald*, July 20th, 1975]

A couple in Staffordshire were driving from Penkridge to Slittingmill one night. Their children were with them. The wife saw a small figure run across the road before them, followed by two more, which she described as looking like hairy trolls. Their estimated height was 4', they were unclothed, had hook noses and hunchbacks. They stood and looked at the car and at length advanced upon it. The adult occupants saw them, but the children were asleep. What happened next, the couple could not remember. Some time after, they remembered that the little hominids were gone and their car started perfectly. They felt they had undergone some sort of experience, but could not remember what it was, from the time the little creatures had advanced on them. The children had apparently slept through everything. [Redfern/Vaudrey, pp. 83-4].

Diminutive humanoids were reported outside Lautoka Methodist Missionary School, Fiji. [Eberhardt, Vol. II, p.572]

1976

John Salter saw a tiny human near Glen Rushen on the Isle of Man.

A car filled with teenagers coming from Glencolumbkille in Ireland by night saw unusual lights and little people. [WL]

1977

Police Constable David Swift observed a bank of fog near Stonebridge Avenue, East Hull (Humberside). Then he saw dancing persons, one a man in a sleeveless jerkin, two women in white dresses with bonnets and shawls. They seemed to be dancing in a circular motion. [F]

Ned Grimm went into wooded land in New York state. Shortly

after entering the trees, he had a strange, tingling sensation. Then he noticed the countryside about him seemed different from what he remembered. There was a strange green tinge in the sky and it had ceased to be overcast. He came on grey cliffs which should not have been there. He heard strange music and, rounding a bend, saw a small waterfall. There four little men were playing pipes, while a fifth was collecting water in a jug. He took a picture with his camera. The little men went away.

He tried to return to his car and walked around for about an hour. Then he saw it through the trees and the strange tingling struck him again. Turning around, he found the strange country had vanished. He thought he had been gone for about three hours, but his watch showed it had been a mere thirty minutes.

When he had his photographs developed, the one showing the Little Men did not come out. [LP]

1978

Kim Pompey Del Rio (aged 13) of Milwaukee was sick and lying on a couch looking out of the window. She saw two little people about 8" high. Their skin was greenish. They may also have had greenish clothes. Although she could not hear them, she could see the beings were laughing at her. [I]

A man looking for his cat came on a cave near Parliament Street, Toronto. He found the cat dead in the cave. A creature covered in hair, about 3' in height, appeared and said, "Go away! Go away!" He went.

1979

The incident at Wollaton Park, Nottingham, must surely stand out amongst fairy sightings. Wollaton is a 500 acre park with much wildlife, including two herds of deer. On October 29th at twilight, a group of about four children approached a fenced-off area of the park. There they saw about 30 small cars, each containing two little men, driving around. The *Fortean Times* (No. 31) says they were bubble-like. (The cars, not the men.) The little men were about half the size of the children, who were aged 8-10. The men had long white beards tipped with red, though one child said the beards were black. Do we ascribe the discrepancy here to the crepuscular light? Their headgear looked like bobble hats. They had blue upper garments and yellow tights. They chased the children, but only in fun, as they could have caught them if they wished. There were discrepancies in accounts of the colour of the cars, perhaps again due to the light. The next morning the school Headmaster questioned the children thoroughly about the incident. Once it became publicised, other persons came forward saying they had seen such beings in the park. The children themselves said they had seen them before, in the school holidays. [F; FT]

1980

A hiker named Don amongst the Adirondacks of upper New York state saw one little man rescue another, who had fallen into the river, by leaning down from an overhanging tree. [LP]

1980s

The child in this story could be either male or female, so I am referring to it as male, as that seems likelier. The incident happened in Perth (Western Australia). The child, then about 6 years of age, was playing in bush land, when he espied a little man like an Aborigine, about 13" tall, clad only in a loincloth. The small man threw a spear, which hit the child in the foot. [PAC]

About 1980 a married couple saw in Donegal a little man about 2' tall wearing a hat. He was smoking a pipe. [WL]

1983

In the city of La Plata, Argentina, green men were reported near a house. One witness said one had flung a brick in his direction. They were, he claimed, like wrinkled old men. One witness claimed they had a single eye each. Suspicion that they came from a well in the garden of the house was current.

1986

A group in the Magonia Swamps Nature Reserve, Durban, South Africa, saw little people of an ethereal, light composition. There seemed to be about 20-30 of them. The onlookers saw them for about ten seconds, then ran. The story was written by Paul de Fleuriot, one of the group. [PAC]

1988

Leslie, a correspondent of Your True Tales (paranormal.about.com – June 2004) claimed to have woken up to see a room full of little people. They were about 3' tall. She described their heads as pointed. [PAC]

1992

On the Aran Islands off the western shores of Ireland, a 15-year old boy beheld two beings, neither much taller than a metre, fishing in the sea. They jumped up and vanished. The boy found a pipe which they had left behind. This he procured, but it later vanished. Readers are warned that when witnesses give accounts of measurement such as height, it can be quite easy to be mistaken. The two beings were talking in Irish. [PND]

1993

A hairy dimunutive human-like being was seen at Bella Vista Itaque, Paraguay. [I]

1994

John L. Hall and a friend in Glen Auldyn, Isle of Man, apparently heard music and tinkling voices. John felt things going fuzzy in his vision and seems to have undergone the beginnings of a panic attack. The pair took photographs and one seemed to show a green man on a pedestal, strange of aspect, in tree branches. [FS]

One J. Barnet, returning from Askham Bog, a nature reserve in Yorkshire, saw, in daylight, people about 4' tall apparently putting on a golf course. Our witness hid behind a tree and on emergence found they were gone. [FS]

1995

Near Boscobel (Wisconsin) Daniel Klemsrud was walking with his girlfriend, to whom he was about to declare undying love. Then they felt they had become lost and the weather had changed. A mist descended on the couple and they heard the sound of giggling round about. Klemsrud, looking between branches, saw two little men in jumpsuits running into a hole. Each was about 3' in height. Then he realised his girlfriend and he were standing on a mound. The girlfriend, who had already given him a mouthful of abuse, now gave him another and a mental message told him that the experience had shown him her true feelings for him. He received another message as a result of which he tossed coins into an opening in the mound. The mist lifted, the sky cleared and the path which he had been unable to see earlier became visible.

Klemsrud had seen Little People often as a small child. [Steiger]

1996

Katrina H. writes that, when she was eleven years old she lived in an old house in Crockett (California). She was in bed one night and started tapping with her fingers. Then she realised someone else was tapping too. Her bedroom contained a walk-in closet. She looked into it and saw a small person with beady black eyes and a beard, perhaps 2' tall. She ran from the room and told her mother. The mother went to investigate and came back saying it was Katrina's imagination. However, about four years later the mother admitted that she too had seen the little man. [PAC]

Students in Valparaiso, Chile, came upon little men about 30cm tall. The one they took to be the leader threw stones at them. Felipe Guerrero Silva said he had met other little people, who were friendlier. [natural plane.blogspot.com]

1997

On the website *arwensoracle.tripod.com* you can see a photograph taken in this year. It shows what appears to be a diminutive being in the woods west of Sebago Lake (Maine).

A humanoid less than 3' tall but adult was seen by Sheron Joy Rogers as it came around the corner of an old house in Glasgow (Kentucky). It wore a thigh-length upper garment and a hat with a point or peak. [I]

Minnie Simpson of Roswell (New Mexico), in a letter to Robert Goerman, a student of the paranormal, said that in this year she saw what she at first mistook for a dog. Bella, her own dog, made the same mistake. Looking more closely, she saw it was a little man about a foot tall with bushy eyebrows and a grey beard. His upper garment was grey and made of wool. His trousers had a rope belt. His footwear looked like socks, but the witness thought they were in fact boots. The being ran into a tree (which had no entrance) and was not seen again. Bella was very frightened.

The Bredlow family were vacationing on the coast of Oregon. They went out walking and a mist descended on them. They called for their two daughters. One came quickly, but the other, Violet, answered from behind them when she should have been in front of them. She said "they" had carried her. Moreover, Violet had no notion there had been a fog.

After their meal that night, Violet dished out two plates of leftovers, saying "they" must be fed. She had said they were two little people.

They left the food in the storage room, where Violet said the little people lived.

Her father opened the storage room door and saw two rats eating the leftovers. Before he could enter the storage room, the door slammed shut and he could not open it.

Violet's father put down a rat trap and their mother, Margie, heard on the fifth afternoon, an awful scream coming from Violet. She ran to the storage room and opened the door. She saw a little man in green trying to free another from the rat trap. She managed to free the little man. Both little men disappeared. She heard one cry, "If it's rats he wants, it's rats he gets."

The cabin became infested with rats and the Bredlows had to leave. [Steiger]

1999

A diminutive being with pointy ears and a brown body was seen one night by a family in Lima, Peru. They had been awoken by a noise which may have been him jumping off the roof. [JHS]

J.J. Dos Santos of Bangues (Minas Gerais), Brazil had stopped his car to take a rest. He saw, looking through the back window, a diminutive being with a large head. He drove away. [JHS]

About this year in eastern Ohio, two groups resident at a camp went into the woods. Both groups had to return due to a storm, but claimed they were being watched by little people in the woods. They suggested they were brownies.

2000

A startled policeman in Frias, Argentina, came upon what he thought was a child, but it turned out to be a humanoid of unknown nature.

2004

K.T. of Greensburg (Pennsylvania) was in the woods with her husband. There had been heavy snow and the woods seemed somehow different, though this may have been accounted for by the snowy outline of the trees. Then a man resembling a typical elf, with pointy ears, a long nose, very long fingers and a pointed cap stepped out from behind a tree. Its clothes were red and its skin is described as being light lavender.

The percipient had had a previous experience when her two-year-old daughter said there was a man sitting on her stone wall. While she was unable to see a man, the air in that place had seemed to shimmer. [PAC]

2006

The Crichton or Mobile Leprechaun was reported in Mobile (Alabama) in this year. [*Wikipedia*]

2007

This incident happened on October 11th to a witness aged 51. I shall use the masculine pronoun to describe the witness, as the gender is unspecified. He awoke feeling he was being stared at. He opened his eyes to see a small being on the bed. He opened his eyes slightly a number of times, then fully. He saw a little person, perhaps 10" tall, human looking, with large eyes, thick brown hair, a jacket with large lapels and a double row of buttons and dark green trousers. The witness was unsure whether the being was male or female. [FG]

The *Aluxob* (singular *Alux*) are little people in the Mayan folklore of Yucatan, Mexico. Sightings have been reported in modern times by Mayans. On December 30th, 2007, D. Gannon was driving from Merida to Okutzkab in Yucatan. He saw an apparent Alux, about 2' tall, in the bushes. It was muscular, brown but not dark brown and had features which were like those of a human and not hairy. He passed this on to the website *Cryptomundo*. Aluxob are supposed to be naked except for a hat. They are also said to sometimes carry shotguns. Another sighting of an Alux was reported by Xuc, a caretaker at an archaeological site. He claimed the Alux pelted him with pellets, which he kept. (This sighting is undated.) We wonder if they might represent a pygmy race, yet to be found in the wilds of Mexico.

2008

Several teenagers at one o'clock in the morning in the town of General Guemes in Argentina saw a being that looked like a gnome. Others saw it also. It was filmed on a mobile phone/cellphone. [FT: 278]

In October, near Hallowe'en, a motorist and her daughter in Campbell County, Tennessee, drove past what she took to be some kind of manufactured effigy, like a scarecrow, sitting on the roadside. It was wearing a black hat and coat. As she passed it, it turned and looked at her over its shoulder. Its eyes were black and its face wrinkled. [www.trueghoststories.com]

The following incident took place in Akron (Ohio). Lizanne awoke at night to see a man 4' tall with a neon green light surrounding him. He seemed agitated, wringing his hands and looking worried. She went back to sleep. [PAC]

2009

On January 10th at Rocklin (California) after dark the witness had seen a humanoid figure. His dog rushed at it. It flew 10' up into the air and then flew to the fence, on which it landed or hovered above. The figure went on beyond the fence. [JHS]

On February 8th, five witnesses perceived a flying man over Cannock Chase in Staffordshire. Cannock Chase is known for its high strangeness. [JHS]

2010

In Poland, a surprised Pole opened his bedroom door one night to see a diminutive being outside. It was grey and had large black eyes. Frightened, he went back to bed. [ufoinfo/humanoid]

Several Spanish farm workers on a truck encountered a 90cm tall being with pointy ears, large eyes and a large head. It impeded their progress. Then, when it walked away, they continued their journey. [ufoinfo/humanoid]

At a small lake in the vicinity of Orekhovo, near St Petersburg, a woman saw a creature that identified itself as a *leshy*. (Varner, p. 22). For those who are unfamiliar with Slavic legends, the leshy is a protector of wild animals and is sometimes said to have the horns, tail and hooves of a goat. He has green hair growing on him. Sometimes, though not in this case, it is said to grow all over him. The occasional hostile leshy will tickle a man to death. A female leshy is called a *lisunka*.

2011

A duende was reported in Suncho Corral, Argentina. He attacked a schoolboy and then knocked a cyclist off his bike. [FT: 278]

2012

A tiny green man was photographed outside a house in Collieston (Aberdeenshire). The photograph is, however, indistinct. [naturalplane. blogspot.co.uk: October 24th, 2012]

The website *Ghost Hunters Inc* received an e-mail dated April 22nd of this year from a person called David. He said he lived in the countryside on the West Virginia/Kentucky border. He claimed that his house was being plagued by diminutive beings with large oily eyes and lipless mouths, but no other facial features. They would look through windows and try to enter the house. He suspected they came from an abandoned mine nearby. He eventually supplied photographs of footprints allegedly left by the creatures. He tended to think they were extraterrestrials. [frontiersofzoology.blogspot.co.uk]

2013

Three-toed footprints of roughly human size were discovered by boys in Concord (New Hampshire). It was suggested that they were made by *Puckwudgies*, diminutive beings in Amerindian folklore. [frontiersofzoology.blogspot.co.uk]

On August 3rd, two friends were sitting on a bench in Perrien Park, Detroit, at about 9.30 in the evening, when they were set upon by two little men, about 4' in height, who attacked them fiercely. They wore green three-piece suits. Suddenly they ceased their assault and ran off, laughing. [Phantoms and Monsters]

Undated

◆ An English child of 6 years in Canada, whither the family had emigrated, woke up to see half a dozen little men. They asked the child about the toys in the room and were particularly taken with the rabbit, which was used as a zipped pyjama case. [PAC]

◆ A British gypsy said that he had seen a fairy couple. The man was diminutive (1.5'-2'), wore knee-breeches and a waistcoat (=U.S. vest) and top boots. He had a green and yellow handkerchief. The woman had an old fashioned but good quality red dress. She had jet-black hair. Both had dark complexions. [Trigg]

◆ In Peru, a man was drowning but was rescued by four dwarfish creatures covered with green scales. These creatures had three fingers each. [Smith *Bigfoots and Bunyips* p.166]

◆ Bob, a child, was sitting in a doctor's waiting room, when he saw a little man on the ledge. He tapped on the window with his walking stick, waved and smiled. The creature was about 1' tall. This happened on Long Island (NY). [LP]

◆ In the area of Ballymoney, a wee man came out of the local fairy fort. These structures are prehistoric or early remains. He moved in with a family one stormy night and remained as their guest. If local lore is to be believed, he was not the only fairy who moved in with a human family.

    This particular incident seems to have occurred in the late 19th Century. [WL]

◆ Two brothers in Wales were looking through a hole in the wall at a stone where fairies were reputed to dance. In due course they saw them. The brothers were children. The fairies were no more than two feet in height. Their clothes were of many colours and their caps had peaks. [GP]

◆ A man called Struan Robertson had a number of paranormal experiences. We shall meet him again later on. On Arran, an island off Scotland, he saw fairies playing around sheep and bushes. On another occasion on the same island, he saw fairies on a green footpath. At Loch Rannoch he saw fairies dancing. [F]

◆ This undated account, written by a person called Matthew, is to be found in the website *Fairy Gardens*. He, his girlfriend and a third party were on a camping holiday in Banff National Park, Alberta, Canada. Due to the cold, Matthew couldn't sleep and then he heard noises like fireworks. He became convinced that there were about thirty little men outside, shooting fireworks from their fingers. They had the faces of oldsters and the voices of children. A dog entered the tent and he put it out. He then heard a ripping sound and the front of a spear entered the tent. A voice said that he might use the dog, but he had to leave the box. He knew which box was meant and said they could have it.

In the morning, before he told his companions what had occurred, the girlfriend said she had had a lucid dream. She was in the air over the camp and said the tent was surrounded by little men, who were shooting fireworks from their fingers and had a dog made out of shadows. She landed and saw Matthew. She asked if he were dreaming and he replied in the affirmative. The little men told her that the dance would begin in an hour, but that they should move the tent.

This rather extraordinary story may be of psychological origin in which dreams somehow intertwined. It would be interesting to know if the rent in the tent was still there in the morning. [FG]

◆ An informant told folklorist Robin Gwyndaf that his grandfather had become lost in a mist in Wales. The fairies came to walk by his side to ensure he arrived home. He said they were as high as his knee. He described them as very light of complexion and the most beautiful beings you ever saw. They wore knee-breeches. These were made of blue velvet. [FG]

◆ Another informant told Robin Gwyndaf he had, as a boy, stopped for a smoke. A little man, about three feet tall, with an old face, arrived from the direction of some green bushes. He did not speak. The informant did not remember his departure. [GP]

◆ A Texan electrician [name withheld] of a somewhat sceptical bent, who impresses the reader as hard-nosed, said that when he was a boy he was on vacation, perhaps in Indiana, but this is not made clear. He was staying in a trailer and one night, when he went to the bathroom, he encountered a little man, perhaps 3" tall, who ran across the floor. He was wearing a white tail coat, a hat, black shoes and white socks. The witness said his stepsister also claimed to have seen little people.

◆ Elin, writing from Wales, said that as a university student, she was woken one night. Her head felt fuzzy. She looked out and saw a man about 4' tall, laughing and jumping. He seemed old and was ruddy.

He took a jump and vanished. Elin did not remember the incident for several days. [FG]

◆ An anonymous correspondent of the *Fairy Gardens* website was recovering from a triple heart bypass when he saw what he described as an elf. He had been feeling miserable. The being reassured him. He was wearing a tweed jacket, had short breeches, long socks and black shoes. The patient looked away twice and, when he looked back the second time, the being was gone. Despite the fact that this story lacks dates and details and the writer, like so many, is anonymous, the fact that he took the trouble to write about his experience means we should not simply dismiss it out of hand. It would not do for a scientist, but it is certainly part of the general accumulation of alleged sightings. [FG]

◆ About 1920 Mrs Hardy of New Zealand wrote to Arthur Conan Doyle, telling him that at twilight she once perceived eight or ten figures riding on tiny ponies. The faces of the beings were brown, as were their ponies. If they were wearing clothes, they were tight-fitting. Here again we have reference to diminutive steeds. Indeed, two mini-horses, 16"-18" in height, were reported in the Philippines in the 1970s. Is there a race of diminutive horses in some other dimension, used by diminutive fairies, who occasionally cross into ours? See also the remarks on such horses in an earlier chapter.

◆ Sir Arthur Conan Doyle received a number of letters from those who had seen fairies. Reverend Arnold J. Holmes wrote that he had once seen at night what appeared to be a small army of indistinct figures in gossamer garments. The beings were small. [CF]

◆ Miss Hall of Bristol wrote to Conan Doyle saying that, when she was about 6 or 7, she saw a funny little man playing among the flowers. She could not remember his face. He seemed to be unclad. In colour he was sage green. He was slender and she estimated that his height was about 3". [CF]

◆ Mrs Ethel Enid Wilson of Worthing (Sussex) said she had often seen fairies. Once her nephews and nieces had seen them too. [CF]

◆ Mrs Rose of Southend-on-Sea seems to have seen many fairies in a shrubbery by the sea and in the conservatory of her house, floating about amidst the flowers and plants. [CF]

◆ A friend of folklorist K.M. Briggs, the widow of a clergyman, was sitting in Regent's Park, London. She had injured her foot. Then a tiny man in green appeared. He seemed well disposed and said, "Go home. We promise that your foot won't hurt you tonight." Then he vanished and so did the pain in her foot. She slept well that night.

The same person once caught a glimpse of fairies dressed in flowers dancing on the side of the flower beds. [FTL]

◆ Judy Hart, living in Wisconsin, was lying one morning on her stomach, the pillow over her head to avoid sunlight. She heard giggling. She looked around to see four little persons in a circle holding hands. They were around 18" tall. One disappeared from the group and she felt something on her back and someone was pushing the pillow down on her head. It seems to have been merely an elfish prank. [PAC]

◆ There have been many alleged sightings of *Puckwudgies*, diminutive beings in whom Native Americans believe, in modern times. Three were said to have occurred in Bridgewater State Forest (Mass). In Northern Ohio a witness called Arika, a correspondent of the website New England Oddities, claimed she, her brother and her father saw some when she was a child. Another correspondent claimed Marlow (New Hampshire) was sniving with them. [NEO]

◆ A tommyknocker is said to be in the woods off MacArthur Boulevard (Maryland). In 1906 there was an explosion at the Maryland Gold Mine. At some stage a ghostly looking man with fiery eyes and a 10' tail was seen crawling out of the shaft. Foreman Edgar Ingalls heard of the first sighting when a night watchman refused to work there any more.

◆ A couple sitting on a log in British Columbia were suddenly faced by a small being bereft of clothing, old and wizened, but well muscled. He was about 3.5' tall. His face was brown. He stamped his foot and made an angry motion with one fist. [psican.org]

◆ A creature strange indeed was encountered by Lili Noemi Castillo when a child in Peru. The being had an old man's face, was naked and had long hair down his back. He had no feet, he was floating. [culture potion.blogspot.co.uk]

◆ A correspondent named Lynn claimed to have seen what she called a gnome dressed entirely in white in Puerto Rico. The second time she saw him she asked him his name and he said it was Sebastian Polizar. Lynne was 17 at the time. Her mother saw the gnome later. [PAC]

◆ A correspondent of *Yahoo! Answers* writing in 2009 said he saw what he took to be an elf in Franconia (New Hampshire). A child at the time, he was playing with his brother when he saw a tiny creature, pink-faced with huge black eyes, clad in a green hat and sweater or coat.

◆ On Grand Manan Island (New Brunswick) is to be found a place called Ghost Hollow, south of Dark Harbour. A Little Man has been seen here by motorists on foggy nights. He rushes out of the woods, runs alongside cars and then jumps in front of them. When the motorist brings the car to a speedy halt, no vestige of the Little Man is to be found. [Colombo, *Mysterious Canada* p. 54]

◆ A writer in the Your True Tales section claims that, as a small child in Carrollton (Texas) he saw a little creature, scraggy, wearing a hat with a silver buckle on the front. He was about 3' tall and hunchbacked and looked very old. His fingers were long and boney, his fingernails also being long. The child saw this being from his bed at night. [PAC]

◆ A man named Jeff informed Ron Quinn that he had found an old abandoned house in New York state. From it, he had seen a little man. He discovered what seemed to be a small room under the floor. It contained rags (?a bed), a stone (?chair, table) and an old tin mug filled with water. [LP]

◆ Fifty green men resembling frogs were reported one night in France [Smith *Bunyips and Bigfoots,* p.165]

◆ The Reverend Bruce of Sixpenny Handley (Dorset), being tired, lay down on Bottlebrook Down. He became aware that he was not alone and saw pixies dancing in a circle around him. They were small and they wore leather jerkins. Then they vanished. [R. Newland *Dark Dorset Fairies* p.26]

◆ Bob and Helen Pepper and Toma and Susan Hodgson were camping in Ulster County (New York). They saw a little man in a tree, whom some of them at first mistook for a doll. Then it moved over to sit beside a baby raccoon. After this it leaped away. During the night, they heard the sound of a flute, then the same sound coming from another direction. This unsettled them. In the morning they left. [LP]

◆ Sir Arthur Conan Doyle was fooled by the Cottingley hoax, but, as stated above, he knew people who claimed to have seen fairies. One of these was Tom Cherman who was a fairy hunter in the New Forest, where he set up a shelter, much as a bird watcher might do. He said the fairies varied in height from a few inches to several feet. They are male, female and children. They have varying kinds of clothing. [CF]

◆ The Moxie Mountain Humanoid, 3'-4' tall, was seen on this mountain in Maine.

◆ A woman called Hannah, interviewed by writer Jon Dathen in his book *Somerset Faeries and Pixies* once saw a pixy running from the front door. He wore a black tail coat, black trousers and white spats. Hannah had the intelligent idea that pixies, when seen, might conform themselves to whatever image of them you had in your mind or else your brain would shape the entity into the image you would expect.

A friend of Hannah's named Ruby said she once saw a group of little people. Few were more than 6" tall. They had little carts and wheelbarrows and even some covered wagons, which tiny oxen drew. While some were wearing fine clothes, some were dressed in tatters, some in leaves, moss or feathers, some had acorn helmets. Some were actually naked. Some carried bundles of sticks on their shoulders. Some rode small ponies, and small dogs frisked about the throng. Some carried musical instruments, some bows or spears. She thought some had tails and were furry. Hannah said that tribes with monarchs were wanderers, but orchard pixies, wood elves and hobs were not. She averred human sized fairies mingled with humans at fairs or markets. She claimed to have spotted many.

◆ Renée, writing to the website paranormalist.com, run by John Carlson, said a little man entered her home in Louisiana and stayed for about an entire summer. He resembled an old human and was perhaps a foot in height. He wore a flat cap.

◆ A tiny grey woman was seen sitting in a rockery in West Sussex.

◆ K.M. Briggs revealed a communication from Mrs Mona Smith, telling of an experience her father underwent as a child. He, his sister and another boy had been placed in the care of their grandmother. Another old woman came to visit. She offered to show the children something. They went down to the banks of a stream and, on the side of a hill, saw fairies dancing around a fire. There was no trace of the fire when they checked the next day. Mrs Smith had heard the tale from her father and later on met the other boy, who corroborated it.

◆ Miss J.M. Dunn, driving home one night, felt creepy and saw diminutive creatures moving among the standing stones at Avebury. This was recorded by the folklorist Kathleen Wiltshire in 1973.

◆ Jon Dathen in his book *Somerset Fairies and Pixies* (2010) writes of a witness named Nathaniel who saw one of the little people silhouetted on the branch of an apple-tree, wearing a Phrygian cap. The witness opined he may have been a kind of pixy known as an *apple pixy* or *grig*. Nathaniel also claimed to have had a sighting of a black shadow running on two legs. This black shadow had a tail. [SFP]

◆ An informant named Jenny told Jon Dathen that her brother Tom, as a child, reported seeing a pixy dance. The pixies were very small. The men wore green with red hats, the girls white dresses. Four hairy old men played on pipes and violins. The male pixies looked to some extent like bewhiskered animals, little goats or hedgehogs. He was sure some had tails.

Jenny also said her grandfather sometimes stewed rabbits in the woods with his father. When they partook of them, they were sometimes joined by two little men who spoke a strange language which Jenny's great-grandfather understood. One wore a tricorn hat, one a hat of the kind associated with Robin Hood. One had a squat face, the other a foxy one. Her grandfather said time seemed to stand still while they were there. The trees seemed "odd" as well. [SFP]

◆ John Carlson, webmaster of theparanormalist.com, has an interesting tale to tell of his own experiences as a child in Wellesley (Massachussetts). He was four years old at the time. The room in which he slept was small but boasted a walk-in closet, at the back of which there was a second-storey window. He started to have what might have been dreams, but were as vivid as real memories. He'd wake up during the night to find small figures entering by way of the closet.

These creatures were shorter than John himself, though they may have been physically powerful. Their eyes were shiny like animals'. They glittered in the dark. He thought the beings were hairy or furry, or perhaps dark-skinned. He sensed an animalish quality about them.

The beings would put their hands upon him and float him out of the bed, through the closet and through the window. At this juncture, his memory would fail.

These visits happened frequently for about three years. After that, they occurred less often. The final encounter he remembers was when he was about nine or ten and the family had then moved to Ringwood (New Jersey).

◆ The ELFEN Project in Canada mentions 4'-5' trolls reported from the forest north of Vancouver. Unfortunately, their archive has not been either printed or put online.

◆ Henrick L. writes from Sweden that his girlfriend, when aged seven or eight, saw a tomte in her parents' room. [PAC]

◆ At the woods in Croton (Lancs) there have been in all 44 fairy reports. One such fairy is a benign entity called Shrewfoot, who has saved at least one pedestrian from being run down by a truck.[29]

◆ Michael Carter, staying at an hotel in Ireland, had been spooked by a plastic leprechaun left on his bed. Later, in the men's room, he noticed a little man behind him. It jumped, striking his head and knocking him out. He came to in hospital. His wallet was gone, so everyone assumed he had been mugged. [PAC]

◆ In Monterrey, Mexico, a little boy bent down to change his shoelace. He was about five. He saw a man of about his own size, with brownish skin and a beard. The man signalled to him to be silent. Thinking he was about to be abducted, the boy ran off. The story was sent in by his sister, Mariana. [PAC]

◆ Betty Kirkland (apparently in the US) saw Little People as a child and didn't realise what they were. She was only three and they were taller than she. One was a man, the other a woman. The woman was shocked when Betty saw them, as she wasn't supposed to be able to do so, but the man just laughed and said she had the gift. They gave their names as Acorn and Fluff – perhaps literal translations of these names from another language. She kept seeing them throughout her childhood. Once they saved her from an angry bull, once from a possibly rabid dog and on one occasion they pulled her from water in which she was drowning. As a teenager and adult she would at times of sadness see sparkling lights with which they indicated their presence or hear their laughter. [Steiger]

◆ Nick Marshall encountered a boy whom he knew in a state of some confusion. It transpired he had been taken by little people into Mount Pilchuk, Alaska. There he met a girl who had been abducted 40 years

---

29 metro.co.uk: October 21st, 2010

before. This is to be found on the *Anchorage Daily News* website (May 11th, 2008). A commentator wrote that he had seen such beings in western Alaska. The Yupik, a local tribe of non-Inuit Eskimo, believe in little people called *incenraat* who have been associated with Mount Pilchuk.

◆ Novelist Elizabeth Goudge knew a woman who had seen friendly elves sitting on her stairs. This is not the woman of whom Elizabeth Goudge narrated another experience, whom we shall meet later in this work. [Elizabeth Goudge *Linnets and Valerians* (1964), Epilogue].

◆ When the witness was a seven-year old girl and in bed with a cold, a little man in green ran into her room shouting, "Hello, hello, hello". [LP]

◆ Jon Dathen interviewed a farmer called Frank. Frank told Dathen that, one night, he heard noises downstairs, including, apparently, someone poking the fire. Frank crept down and saw, sitting on the stool in front of the fire, a diminutive being. It actually looked like a hare dressed in clothes and it had long, hairy feet with long toes. Its shirt seemed too small. It had a green waistcoat and some kind of cap. Its face looked like it was a combination of a hare's and a human's and it had long ears. He turned and saw Frank. He had teeth that looked like a hare's. He looked at Frank and said, "Cold!" He ran out of the door. He had a tail that looked quite long. [SFP]

◆ Richard O'Donnell (17) lived in a Minnesota town near a cave supposed to contain trolls. They were probably so designated as most of the inhabitants of the town were of Scandinavian descent. He encountered one one day – he was short and stocky with a long nose. He was very ugly. He attacked O'Donnell, who flipped him on his back. O'Donnell felt the motive for the attack might have been to acquire clothing, as the troll's own was worn. Then, doubtless to O'Donnell's astonishment, the troll grew in size, gaining about 50 pounds and growing from roughly 5'4" to 6'4" and splitting his shirt. O'Donnell ran back to town. [Steiger]

◆ Kay Mullin in her book *The Wondrous Land* (1997) collected a number of accounts of sightings of the Little People in Ireland. Joseph, one of her informants, had seen a number of them at Knockalla (Donegal) on a number of occasions, the first time when he was about eight years old. His grandfather said they were nothing to be frightened of. Sometimes he got as close to them as 15 or 20 feet. They were male and female, but he didn't see any children. They were mostly dressed in red. Their hair was fair, black or brownish. They seemed to at last fade away, like vanishing ghosts.

Joseph also had what may have been a UFO experience. On one occasion when, he assured Miss Mullin, he had not taken drink or medication, he saw an object which could have been a big round building descending. When it passed down out of view, he expected to hear some noise like a crash. He heard nothing. He was well aware that whatever he saw was a huge machine.

Another informant, John, said he once had seen a wee woman in the woods. She apparently came out of nowhere. She was about 2' tall. She wore tartan. When she came nearer to him, John, who was only 13, fled.

A farmer from the Mourne Mountains (Down) saw red clad creatures dancing one night. It was stormy, so he was sure they were not children. A fiddler said they were seen in an area called Quinn's Woods until 1940.

A man named John O'Brien was bulldozing a ditch (?hedge) and needed to remove a stone. He saw behind it a little man, 2.5' tall. He ran off.

◆ The Nage people on the island of Flores, Indonesia, have in their legends a diminutive race called the *Ebu Gogo*. On the small island remains of the small *Homo floresiensis* have been discovered. Surviving populations of them may lie at the root of belief in the Ebu Gogo. They are different in bone structure from *Homo sapiens*.

There are no doubt many more accounts which could be cited.

These accounts, for the most part, would be dismissed by the sceptic on the grounds that they are open to more than one interpretation, which indeed they are. He would be inclined, quite rightly, to treat anonymous accounts from Internet sources with caution. But these accounts indicate a possible fairy reality and he should not close his mind to that possibility. It should be remembered that many people might prefer to remain anonymous to avoid being scoffed at rather than because they were uttering falsehoods.

Chapter Five
CONVENTIONAL faiRIes

tHERE is no actual definition of what a conventional fairy might be and I have used the term as a matter of convenience. In this case, it generally means either a tiny flying being or a being (usually female) of human size. As some of these fairies are connected with light, I have also included sightings of disembodied but apparently living lights. Our mental image of these fairies has been coloured by imagery which is largely based on Victorian illustration and the depiction of fairies in the media.

The White Ladies (French *Dames Blanches*, German *Weisse Frauen*) form a sort of prototype of these beings. They are usually tall and beautiful. Jacob Grimm feels these beings are 'half-goddesses', not always distinguishable from goddesses. These sound rather like the originals of our human-sized fairies. The Germans called this kind of being *itis*. This would equate to Latin *matrona* and the Germans culted deities referred to in Latin as *Matronae*.

In the Netherlands you had beings called *Witte Wieven* who were concerned with health. They lived in the hills. They may have become connected with or even developed from wise women healers who were culted after their deaths.

A White Lady in England is called the White Lady of Hell-Clough in Yorkshire, who is said to rise from a pool and drift across a field.

A difficulty if you spot a White Lady is telling she is a fairy or ghost.

The French White Ladies are associated with Normandy, Lorraine and the Pyrenees. There were also in France Green Ladies (*Dames Vertes*). Their names were derived, not from their skin, but from their clothes.

Related to these are the *mouras encantadas* of Portugal and Galicia, who are generally under a spell that keeps them guarding something and they sit waiting for someone to release them. They comb their hair, which can be golden, black or red, with a golden comb. The term seems to be quite widely used to cover a number of functions they perform and they are credited with the power to shapeshift. They are said to have built forts in the Stone Age and some are said to live in stones.

In eastern Europe the Czech *poludnice* could be an airy white woman or an old woman; the Poles said the same creature was a tall woman with a sickle who would chase people out of the wood; while in Russia they believed in tall beautiful girls in white.

Among the regular fairies we might class the Irish *banshee*, whose name signifies a fairy woman. The banshee would warn of forthcoming death. People claim to have heard her and even to have seen her. Her cry resembles the Irish custom of *keening* (uttering a lament) over a dead person. In the south-west of Ireland the banshee is sometimes called a *badhbh*. This was originally the proper name of an Irish goddess. Before a battle, if you came on Badhbh washing items in a river, it signified your forthcoming death. These days in Irish the word *badhbh* is used as a common noun, signifying the hooded or scald-crow (*Corvus corone cornix*). It is also used to mean a vulture.

Certain families seem to have had special banshees attached to them. The O'Brien banshee, Aoibheall, had 25 other banshees attendant on her.

The term banshee migrated to America. In Ohio, a banshee is a little old woman with long hair. However, in that state, the term is also applied to men 2' tall with red hair. They have tails with which they hang from trees.

A Scottish variant of the banshee, found in the Highlands, was the *caoineag*. Brittany too had its version, the *tunnerez noz*.

In W.W. Gill's *Third Manx Scrapbook* (1963) we learn that the author was told by a lighthouse keeper how his father and another man saw a woman dressed in white near the church. The man approached her, but she seized him by the arm and spun him round until he was dizzy. Her finger marks remained on the man's arm until the day of his death.

In Italy, fairies seem to be noted from the Middle Ages. Of human size, they often wore conical hats, called *hennin*. They may have replaced the nymphs of ancient lore. Fairies were sometimes godmothers (*comari*).

A contributor to the *Fortean Times* message board (February 15th, 2008) said she was walking on the Fairy Hill at Aberfoyle, celebrated as being near the home of the Reverend Kirk, when she noticed a couple in Highland dress. They stepped off the path and vanished. She compared their disappearance to walking through an invisible door. Fairies?

Going back to 1977, Janet and Colin Bord in their book *Modern Mysteries of Britain* report a case of a camper in Scotland who, at Clowbridge Reservoir, saw an 8' tall person with a beard and a white robe. Again, one can only speculate on whether he was one of the fairy race.

The Scottish *gruagach* is described as a long-haired female who looks after cattle. There are smartly dressed male *gruagachs* too. However, they should be distinguished from the Irish *gruagach*, a different kind of creature altogether, perhaps a kind of ogre in origin.

One might ask who the husbands of these human-sized fairies were. In Scotland the term *elf* was used to mean a male fairy and this was found in England too if we go by Spenser's *Faerie Queene*. In France the word *Fé* as contrasted with female *Fée* was used. In the Saint-Malo region we find *Fétaud*.

But what of the Tiny Fairies, who are also conventional, such as J.M. Barrie's Tinkerbell? These are by no means unknown.

The website *Fairy Gardens* is helpful here, as people send in accounts of fairies they believe they have seen. The anonymity of correspondents is generally protected, for the obvious reason that otherwise they would have to put up with endless and irritating chaffing from unbelieving friends.

Thus one writer with name withheld assures us that what she has to say is not a joke. In her bathroom she saw a white fairy with a white frock and wings. The sighting lasted only for a second. She heard the wings flap. In 1998 she saw a fairy in her computer room. It combined shades of blue and was in a bubble. In some photographs taken of this correspondent (whom I have assumed to be female, but perhaps was male) little blue lights appear next to her face.

Awakened by dog barking on Midsummer Eve, Erica tells us she looked out and saw a small being floating over some dogs.

Lizzie, who hails from Brisbane in Australia, could hear giggling from the bushes in her garden. She went to look and had to look for some time before she spied a fairy. It was blue with bright purple eyes.

In Wales a five year-old child and his mother saw a fairy sitting on a rock in a puddle. She even accepted cake from the child. She waved and flew off.

A correspondent of *Fairy Gardens* (male, 35) from Britain claims he was in the Forest of Dean when, approaching St Anthony's Well, he saw a white figure, almost translucent, human in shape, about 5" tall. It had wings like a butterfly's and flew off, close to the ground.

Marlene, on the website *paranormal.about.com* (Your True Tales – February, 2004) claims she saw glowing lights in the shape of balls. She then saw they were fairies, one male, the other female. The female landed on her hand. Then they were frightened by one of her children coming out of the house.

A correspondent writing to the same site was camping in her back garden. She heard a sound like butterfly wings. Looking out of her tent, she saw a tiny person with tiny red wings. She gave off a blue sparkle.

Phyllis Bacon of Croydon took a photograph of her garden at night, without paying attention to what she was photographing. To her amazement, when the photograph was developed it showed a tiny flying humanoid with wings. The photograph can be seen on the *Mail Online* website.

An office worker in Exeter, looking out of his fifth or sixth floor window saw something that looked like a tiny winged person swinging on a swing in a tree. The person had wings like those of a dragonfly. The story appears on the website *About.com Paranormal Phenomena*.

In the 1970s Jacqui Ford of London, then a child, awoke to see a diminutive female fairy wearing a silver dress and sporting long blonde hair at the end of her bed. It disappeared down a plughole in a basin in her room.[30]

A correspondent called Danica claimed that, when she and her daughters were renting a caravan at El Cajon (California), she saw a fairy out of the corner of her eye. She (the fairy) was sprinkling gold dust around her and was about 3' tall. One of her daughters also saw the fairy.

A correspondent of About.com (Your True Tales, December 2006) saw, at the age of eight, in Pennsylvania, a fairy about 3" tall in a white dress. Her hair was reddish brown. This happened about 2001. Her friends came to see fairies too. Her mother had seen a fairy as a child.

A woman told Rosemary Guiley that she was driving along an unlit country road in New England in 2006 when she saw a tiny fairy with wings which had a design on the upper part. She wore clothes, but no shoes. Her hair was blonde. She smiled at the driver. Guiley repeated the story in her book *Fairies* (2010).

A correspondent who wrote to *Fairy Gardens* in 2004 said at the age of six and seven, she awoke to find three fairies dancing lightly on her (or possibly his) stomach.

---

30 N. Arnold *Mystery Animals of Britain: London*

Laura, writing to the same website, when she was eight years of age, heard tapping at the window. She saw a light which wrote on the window, "Hello, I'm OK." (There may have been frost on the window pane, as there was snow outside). Opening the window, she saw eight fairies sitting on the closed bin.

While the two accounts given above may, of course, have resulted from confused childhood memories, this is not to say that such was definitely the case. Children seem especially susceptible to sightings. Perhaps they have some special faculty dulled or lost in later life.

Returning to larger fairies, the webmistress of artofhacking.com says that she saw a fairy of tall size in Ireland in 1984. She was wearing what looked like a red tutu. The fairy, not the webmistress.

In 2005 witness Johnathan Fennell and his friends were sitting at sunset at the back porch of a house in Chicora (Pennsylvania). They heard a ping, as though something had knocked against a flowerpot. He then saw a human headed creature that looked like an enormous bat or moth with long pointed ears. It flew skywards, unfurling its wings to reveal a human female body. A green glow came from her and her hair seemed green. The body and wings looked as though they were covered in white hair. She was perhaps a foot tall. She flew into the woods.[31]

A contributor to Your True Tales (About.com Paranormal, January 2004), said that, in 2004, she and her family were passing a house in San Antonio (Texas) when she saw fairies fluttering by the mailbox. One of them looked at her and they flew into the grass.

It is interesting that accounts of human-sized fairies perceived by modern persons seem to be few. Perhaps the reason is simply that modern people don't imagine fairies as human-sized and, if they encounter a human-like paranormal person, they report it (if they report it at all) as a ghost or even alien. They could, of course, mistake it for an ordinary human. (The woman who lives next door might be a fairy – have you ever seen her flying around her house at night?)

Going back to fairy student Dermot MacManus, we find that his aunt, who was also an author, was told a curious story by an old woman about an event which had happened when the latter was eighteen. She and other girls were sitting by a lake when they heard horses approaching. They assumed a party of the upper classes was drawing near. The girl then saw that the group consisted of eight men

31 naturalplane.blogspot.co.uk

and women with bright clothes and their saddles and bridles coloured. They seemed to be of normal human size. Instead of riding to the local "Big House", they turned to the right and rode to the local fairy fort, surrounded by thorns and presumably on a hill. They rode into the earth. (I suspect the hillside is meant.) Their demeanour was identical with that of riders entering a stable gate. The girl told her friends in a dégagé manner that it was only some fairies going into the fort.

Jon Dathen was told by his interviewee Hannah that her husband had once seen an old woman in the woods, who vanished before his eyes. He took this to be a fairy.

Author and webmaster Robert Newland claimed to have encountered a fairy which he termed a *dryad* (tree nymph) at Lewiston Hill in Dorset. He had another fairy experience: when listening at a barrow (burial mound) for fairy music, he and a friend heard a single high-pitched tone.[32]

Christopher of North Carolina wrote to *Fairy Gardens* enclosing a photograph he took of what might, on close inspection, prove to be fairies. He enclosed two similar photographs from his friend Sabrina.

A correspondent named Amos said that when he and his wife were out walking the dog at Stourport on Severn (Hereford and Worcester), they saw a diminutive being, 3'-4' tall, with a head that seemed disproportionately large in comparison to its body. [FT: 181]

Fairy-like beings taking the form of globes of light have been reported by a personage known to me who visits rustic sites by night. They are not mere meteorological or geological phenomena, as they seem to have minds of their own. They seem to exercise proprietary rights over the fields they occupy, but are generally friendly, giving an impression of being welcoming. However, on one occasion such a globe proved hostile and my informant and a friend were chased by it out of a field.

In Cajun folklore, certain lights are regarded as fairies and have been since the 1920s. Just what they are is not certain. They are called *feufollets*.

Of course, these accounts generally do not reveal ultimate sources, but even if only some of them are true, it shows the existence of these creatures.

---

32 R. Newland *Dark Dorset Fairies*

Chapter Six

fairy animals

tHIS short chapter will take a look at animals of a fairy nature. We shall start with the Irish Púca, a creature which may not be in truth an animal at all, for it is a shape shifter. One tradition says that the true nature of the púca is an old man wearing rags. However, he is usually seen as a black horse, a donkey or a goat. Dermot MacManus speaks of him as a big black dog, but one wonders if this is the same creature.

The website essortment.com claims there was a recent report of a púca in County Down. This occurred in the townland of Carricknaderriff. There was a tradition of a speaking horse in County Fermanagh until recently, but whether this was a púca remains uncertain.

Dermot MacManus tells us that in 1928 in County Derry, a Mr Martin was fishing. He saw, in a local river, a huge black animal, whose nature he could not work out. The possibility of a panther appears to have occurred to him. When he looked at him, he thought the animal almost human in intelligence. The animal bared its teeth at him and eventually passed out of sight. This leaves me wondering if Mr Martin might have seen a *dobharchú*, a legendary giant otter of Irish folklore. One was supposed to have killed Grace Connolly in 1722 in County Sligo. This creature was also the subject of belief in Scotland, where there is a Loch nan Dobhrachan. In the English of Scotland it is called the *king otter*.

In Ashby-de-la-Zouche in 1990 a witness saw what she believed to be a púca. It looked like a piglet, but it had a pointy nose and she could not discern a tail. It was on a pelmet. [PND]

Richard Freeman, intrepid explorer and horror-story writer, has an account of a creature he suggests is a púca. In 1997 in County Down Louise Donnan and her niece Clare saw ahead of them what they first mistook for a sheep. Then they saw its coat looked like rags rather than wool. It caused them to feel revulsion. It came level with Clare's window and they could see its eye. From the eye Louise felt it had a mind other than an animal's. Clare drove away quickly. The animal ran beside the car, banging it. After a while it stopped.

The púca will, in equine or asinine shape, pick you up on its back and will give you a rollicking ride, but will not otherwise harm you. However, should you venture to Scotland, beware the galloping kelpie.

The kelpie looks like a horse, but is generally thought to live in a body of water and you can tell a kelpie by its mane, which drips all the time. That a horse is not its true form is asserted by those who maintain it is a shape shifter. However, should you mount this beast, it will dive into the water and eat you. Its skin resembles that of a seal. If you can seize its bridle, you're in luck, for then it has to obey you. The kelpie can also appear as a hairy man, who will jump out of cover and crush you to death. As an explanation of the kelpie, it strikes me that it may be something like the horse-eels of Irish legend and in fact be some unknown species which might be mistaken for a pony that appears sometimes in fog or mist on the lochside. A curious creature called the *each uisge* (water horse) has been reported from many Scottish lochs, notably Loch Ness, leading to the suspicion that perhaps an unknown phocid with a horse-like head may lie behind the reports. The Loch Ness Monster is, if it really exists, is said to be much larger than a horse, but there may be smaller specimens. These could occasionally in misty weather, for which Scotland is famous, have been mistaken for ponies.

I have been using in this paragraph one unknown to explain another, which I shouldn't really do. But I've done it.

The *tatter-foal* is a goblin of the east of England. He will appear like a small horse or colt and his coat is rough, whence his name.

In the Shetland Islands, the *njuggle* (or *noggle*) is the equivalent of the kelpie. The Scandinavian *bachhasten* behaves in a similar way. Out in Croatia you have *Orko*, a donkey in gaseous form. He will insert himself between your legs, solidify and carry you away – but not too far away.

Scotland also boasts the *cat sìth* (fairy cat) and the *cù sìth* (fairy dog). The former is supposed to be black, with a white spot on its throat, the latter large and green. A man who discovered the paw prints of the *cù sìth* said they were as large as his outspread palm. The *cù sìth* was much feared in Scotland. The *cat sìth* may be based on sightings of the Kellas cat. This is a type of wild animal discovered in Scotland and it conforms to the description of the *cat sìth*. It was first described in 1983. It is descended from both Scottish wildcats and domestic cats and nobody seems to know how long it has existed in the wild. There is another kind of Scottish fairy cat, green in colour.

One of the most ferocious supernatural cats of legend was the terrible Cath Palug, which features in Welsh legend. Its name actually means "the clawed cat", but it in time became part of a story in which it was the property of a man called Palug. It has been suggested that it was a leopard owned by a Welsh prince. This explanation is unlikely. In the poem *Pa Gur*, the cat is mentioned in the same breath with "lions" which seem to be nothing other than miscellaneous monstrous preternatural creatures. The creature entered French romance as *Capalu*. His preternatural character is perhaps emphasised by the fact that in the romance *Bataille Loquifer* he is a human being called *Kapalu*, a servant of Morgan La Fée. That the Cath Palug was no ordinary cat is borne out by the fact that his mother was the sow, Henwen.

The Basques believed that, underground, there dwelt a red bull of a preternatural stamp. This creature was called the *zezengorri*. They also believed in the *White Blackbird* which would restore sight.

In the folklore of Cape Breton Island we find the *aog*, a creature resembling a mustelid, which causes trouble at wakes.

Our old friend Gervase of Tilbury mentions the *Grant*, which takes the form of a colt. This creature is benevolent. It makes the dogs bark to warn people if there is a fire.

Another helpful animal known in Perthshire is the Lame Goat (*Gabhar Bacach*) which will provide enough milk to satisfy any family. Across the Atlantic in the Pine Barrens of New Jersey you will find, we are told, the helpful White Stag, which will guide you if you are lost. One story is that he prevented a stagecoach from going into the Batsto River when the bridge was damaged.

Let us go to the sewers of London – not everybody's ideal destination, I realise – and mention two strange animals down there that might be termed supernormal. The first is the King Rat. By this I want to make clear I do not mean a rat-king, which is a number of rats which have become tied together by their tails and cannot free themselves. The King Rat is one that seems distinct from the others. It is larger, paler and has a bodyguard of lesser rats. On its arrival, other rats make way for it. Whether this beast is accorded such deference in reality or whether witnesses misinterpret what they see, I cannot, of course, say.

The other creature was the Queen Rat. In the 19th Century the London sewers were frequented by men called *toshers*, who would fish in the sewage for anything of value they could find. Sometimes, legend had it, they would be approached by a beauteous human female. She would perhaps mate with them. But she was no human, but the Queen Rat in disguise, a fact betrayed by her animal-like eyes and the fact that she had claws instead of toenails. Afterwards, if the tosher had children by his wife, they would each have one blue eye and one grey one. Because rats are strange creatures, I wouldn't rule out the possibility of something like the King Rat existing in reality. The Rat Queen sounds more like a piece of erotic imagination.

The *Colepixy* of Dorset is a goblin in equine form. It will lure a rider onto its back and dash around with him, eventually throwing him off. In 1967 the Bruce Family of London were staying at Redlands Farm Caravan Site when Mrs Bruce was awakened by a grey shape with a horse's head trying to pull off her bed covers. She screamed and the creature vanished.

Strange animals are sometimes reported from mines. One of these is the preternatural Green Pig, which is believed to dwell in mines in Bolivia. The Gob Monster, in mines in Illinois, will attack miners when their lights go out. Or so it is said.

We might conclude with the Translucent Turkey, which has allegedly been seen in Wales and which is described in C. Saunders *Into the Dragon's Lair* (2003). It is supposed to be a huge bird that twirls around. All the time it twirls, it increases in size. This process fills the onlooker with fear and he generally absquatulates before the bird stops twirling, so what happens then remains unkenned. One wonders if this is in fact nothing more than some meteorological phenomenon, but then again, perhaps it isn't.

Chapter Seven

water fairies

WE will start with a type of water spirit which I am quite sure does not exist, but which I include for the sake of completeness. It is said the Boto, a dolphin found in the Amazon, can change himself into a male human, in effect, a wereman. In this guise, he will join parties and, fully dressed, he will play the saxophone. These *encantados,* as they are called, are virtuosi on that instrument. They will become involved with women, but any woman whom an encantado makes pregnant is believed to have acted involuntarily and is therefore not blamed for her condition. Now, there was a handy excuse, if ever I heard one.

Let us turn to the Mermaid and her less well-known consort, the Merman. Just to make matters clear, in a number of languages the word employed for a mermaid is *sirena,* but mermaids should not be confused with the sirens of classical mythology. These were supposed to have dwelt on the island of Anthemoessa and to have lured sailors with their irresistible song to their watery doom. They are described as having the heads of female humans and the bodies of birds.

The mermaid is a somewhat different creature, endowed with a tail in lieu of legs. In Scottish legend, some can take these appendages off, revealing legs underneath. Mermaids, you would think, are an impossibility. Yet, surprising as it seems, there are so many accounts of them to which witnesses have testified, that I cannot help but feel we must allow for the possibility of truth behind the legend.

A popular way of explaining mermaids is by saying they are the result of sighting dugongs and manatees. The only trouble with this is many mermaids have been reported in cold northern oceans unfrequented by manatee and dugong. We must then ask what kind of creature lies behind the reports, but we must first take a look at some accounts of actual sightings.

◆ Going back to 1403, when the dykes burst at Edam (Netherlands), a stranded mermaid was discovered. She lived with humans for 15 years and, although she was taught to spin, she never spoke.

◆ In 1608 Henry Hudson was making a voyage trying to discover the North-East Passage. Two of his crew espied a mermaid off the coast of Russia. She was human-sized with long, black hair and her tail was compared with that of a porpoise.

◆ In 1610 Captain Whitbourne claimed he saw a mermaid in St James Harbor, Newfoundland. In the same year, a mermaid approached the coast at Bayonne and was driven back by poles.

◆ Indian legends speak of mermaids living in the Merced River in California.

◆ In 1811 John McIsaac, farmer, from the Kintyre Peninsula, Scotland, saw a mermaid whose height he estimated from 4'-5'. After some hours she entered the water. What seems to have been the same creature was seen by a woman named Kathleen Loymachan.

◆ In 1826 a farmer and his family in Wales saw, out at sea, a short-haired mermaid who was very beautiful. Her body was absolutely white. She was upright and they could not be sure if she boasted a tail.

◆ In 1830 a small mermaid, who may, in fact, have been a mer-child, was spotted off the coast of Benbecula in Scotland. She was struck by a stone, thrown by a boy. Some days later, she was washed ashore. The upper part of her body looked like that of a small child with a developed breast. The lower part looked like a salmon, but lacked scales. The local sheriff evidently thought she looked enough like a human to be given a proper human burial in a coffin.

◆ In 1857 the *Shipping Gazette* reported a sighting of a mermaid by a sailor, who was much taken with her good looks.

◆ It was believed that certain caves on the Aberdeenshire coast were occupied by mermaids and a fisherman claimed to have spoken to one there in the 1870s.

◆ In 1898 a number of mermaid sightings were reported off the Orkney Islands.

◆ Remaining in Scotland, in 1900 Alexander Gunn saw a beautiful mermaid on the shore, awaiting the tide. Her hair was reddish, her eyes blue-green.

◆ A good way to the south two fishermen near Darsen Island, South Africa, saw a creature conforming in every way to the traditional description of a mermaid in 1921.

◆ About 1934 a report came in of a mermaid from the coast of Chile. She was said to have had green hair and luminous eyes.

◆ In 1947 a Scottish fisherman saw a mermaid floating by on a herring box. When she saw him, she dived into the water.

◆ In 1960 two farmers in Ashdee, in the south-west of Ireland, reported that they saw a mermaid and were quite sure it was not a seal.

◆ In 1961 a mermaid was seen off the Isle of Man by a number of people including the Mayoress of Peel.

◆ A mermaid with long blonde hair was reported off Victoria (British Columbia) in 1967.

◆ In 1988 Robert Foster was scuba diving off the Florida coast when he was attacked by what looked like a traditional mermaid, half-woman, half-fish. Foster was a professional, so his testimony is well worthy of consideration. She looked so full of hate that he was sure she meant to kill him. He gave up diving after this, no more wishing to brave such dangers and I blame him not.

◆ Going to more southerly waters, Captain Wedell's Antarctic expedition of 1822-4 stopped at Hall Island, leaving some stores there, with a sailor to guard them. This matelot said he saw a reddish mermaid, who lifted head and shoulders out of the water.

◆ R. Mellaart was stationed on Morotai Island, now in Indonesia, during the Second World War. He discovered some natives had captured a mermaid. She looked completely human above the waist, except that she had six fingers her hands. Mellaart found her ugly and said she had a long nose. The tail resembled a dolphin's with a double fin. He went for help. When he returned she was dead. The natives told him that these creatures were eaten as food on occasion.

◆ In 1991 a mermaid was reported off the coast of Australia.

◆ In 2007 a mermaid was reported by small children at Quistochoca Lake, Peru. She had golden hair and a thin tail. She seemed to be well known in the local area and had never done anyone harm.

◆ In the balmy waters of the Mediterranean, at the Israeli seaside town of Kiryat Yam, Shlomo Cohen saw what he took to be a sunbather. He then discovered it was a mermaid. When she dived into the sea, her tail was readily discernable. She seems to have made a number of appearances at sunset, where she performed tricks for the delectation of the onlookers. Her appearances continued for some months. These events occurred in 2009.

◆ There seems to be a possible special race of mermaids reported from the southerly parts of Africa. Cleo Rosin and her mother lived on the Zimbabwean side of the Zambezi. One day in 1951 they saw on an island in the river a naked white woman with long black hair and a tail.

◆ Hernanus Fourie claimed that, as a child, he had seen a woman sitting at the front of a waterfall in the Karoo region of South Africa. She waved to him before disappearing into the water.

◆ In the year 2000 at Charmwood, Zimbabwe, Marko Batau saw a naked white woman with a fish's tail in the Hunyani River on three occasions, once bathing a baby.

◆ In the South African newspaper *The Herald West Cape News* (January 15th, 2008) we find a story of the Kaaiman, a mermaid that is supposed to be white with black hair and red eyes. She was seen on the banks of the Buffelsjags River in the Western Cape by Daniel Cupido and others. Cupido heard a loud sound and found the mermaid thrashing about in the water. He went to help her, but she faced him with her eyes, putting him into a trance-like state and he felt drawn towards her. He called others to help him and thereby broke the trance. She then seems to have departed. M. Jantjies, local tourist officer, said she knew a number of people who had seen the Kaaiman.

◆ On the island of Guernsey in the English Channel there was a fish-tailed mermaid referred to as the *Guernsey Siren*. These creatures, however, were supposed to have the faces of old crones.

◆ The Micmacs of Eastern Canada believed in a kind of mermaid called a *sabawaelnu*. It is said that a juvenile was found stranded on the shore and returned to the sea by an Indian.

◆ Ubiquitous Fortean Nick Redfern reports he once interviewed a family for the *Chase Post* (now defunct), a Staffordshire newspaper which takes its name from the mysterious Cannock Chase, where the strange seems an everyday occurrence. This family avers that they once came upon the naked dead body of a woman on the side of the road, with her legs fused together below the knee, in mermaid fashion.

Mermen have never seemed to share the attraction of mermaids, for obvious reasons. Perhaps the earliest figure who could possibly be so described is the classical god Triton. He was the son of Poseidon/ Neptune and he was human to the waist down and a dolphin below. He was associated with Lake Tritonis, a large body of water, now dried up, in North Africa. Mermen off the British coast did not have the best of reputations and it was said in one folktale they would eat their own children, which is a somewhat dastardly thing to do. During the reign of King John (1199-1216), we are told by Ralph of Coggeshall (13th Century) that a wild man, bald but of human configuration, was captured at sea. He seems to have adjusted reasonably well to life ashore, but his favourite food was raw fish. He escaped, but returned, then escaped for a second time. He never spoke. He does not seem to have been a merman as such: he certainly lacked a tail. If he was a normal man, one has to ask how he survived at sea.

Lars Thomas records the capture of a merman in Oslo Bay in 1619. There were two royal counsellors present. The merman spoke Danish and uttered threats regarding the outcome if he were not released at once, so they set him free.

A merman was reported by a Jesuit missionary in Canada in 1675. Henry Reynolds (18th Century) claimed to have encountered a fierce-looking merman, with a sharp nose and a tail. A family in 19th Century Scotland claimed descent from a merman, who had mated with a local. Sailors saw a merman from a ship (*Aberdeen Chronicle*, 20th August, 1814). They said he was human to the waist, but couldn't see if he boasted a tail. The Scandinavian merman, the *havmand*, has a green or black beard and hair.

A most extraordinary account is furnished by Waldron in his *History and Description of the Isle of Man*, cited above. He writes of a man who was let down into the water in a "machine". Through the window of this he saw an underwater city which had streets and large squares with crystal pyramids and a beautiful building made of mother of pearl. He made the "machine" roll towards this and enter it. He found himself in a very spacious room containing an amber table surrounded by chairs. The floor was made of rough diamonds, emeralds, rubies and pearls. He said they were cemented by time and could not be unfastened. The line at this stage was being pulled up. He saw comely mermen and beautiful mermaids. This episode allegedly occurred when England was ruled by Oliver Cromwell's Commonwealth (1649-1660) and few if any ships visited Man.

How should we evaluate this astonishing tale, which is presented as true? First, we must consider the nature of the machine. The diving bell had been known from ancient times, but an improved version had been made by Franz Kesler in 1616. This may have been the appliance involved. The purpose of the exercise may have been the discovery of wrecked ships containing treasure. That the machine was actually lowered into the water seems to be fairly well established, but for the story of the city and the merfolk we have only the word of its doughty denizen. Perhaps he was hallucinating, perhaps not. Some day someone may do some diving in the area to find out the truth.

What are we to make of all these accounts of merbeings? A clue is perhaps to be found in the description of the tails. While usually described as fishtails, sometimes they have been described as those of a dolphin or porpoise. This seems to indicate we are dealing here with some kind of mammal, with mammalian features not alone above, but also below, the waist. Could it be that some form of humanoid evolved with its lower limbs fused, producing a tail rather than legs? It should be remembered that Alistair Hardy (1896-1985) suggested that the ancestors of humans spent some of their time evolving in the water. Although this idea was taken up with gusto by Elaine Morgan (born 1920), it is regarded as not proven by scientists; but that doesn't mean it didn't happen. Could a branch of these pre-humans have broken away from the others and taken to the sea? One may scoff at such an idea, but the sea is very large and one cannot say with certainty what is in it.

In Ireland and Scotland there is the belief that certain seals are humans under their skins, which they sometimes doff. If you seize a selkie's skin, she is your captive. However, selkie stories seem to the present writer to be variants of mermaid stories. They may arise from the odd sealskin-clad Lapp in a kayak being carried south.

Let us leave the oceans for a time, as they can very well get on without us, and take a look at fairies in lakes. These are not mermaids or at least they do not have caudal appendages. If we go to Wales we find that there was once a group of physicians who were celebrated under the name of the Physicians of Myddfai. Their historicity is established. The last of their number seems to have been John Jones, surgeon, who died in 1739. Various families claimed descent from them. However, there is a curious legend about their origin.

A young man, tending his mother's cattle, way back in medieval times, encountered a fairy maiden at Llyn y Fan Fach. He at length married her after a curious courtship, in which he offered her bread each day for a number of days, which she kept refusing until it was baked just right. He also had to tell which of two identical lake-dwelling sisters she was in order to obtain her lake-dwelling father's consent. When the wedding took place the young man had been warned that, if he struck her three causeless blows, instant divorce would follow. Over the years he struck her three causeless blows accidentally and she returned to her watery abode.

The couple had had a number of sons by this time. When one of them, Rhiwallon, was walking by the shore of the lake, his mother surfaced and told him he was to become a great physician, as would his family, and this proved to be the case. Rhiwallon is an historical character and he became personal physician to the Lord Rhys of Deheubarth (reigned 1155-97). The medical reputation of the family became established.

Here we have the record of a man whose mother was actually supposed to be a fairy. Unfortunately, it is quite possible the fairy part of the story was a later addition. It is not found in written record until it appeared in print in 1861. While it is not impossible that it preserves a tradition that had persisted in oral lore from the Middle Ages, it cannot be said to be anything like conclusive evidence for the existence of the fairies. It is said that, in the region of Myddfai today, there is a higher than usual proportion of beautiful girls, who owe their looks to being descended from the lake maiden.

Another family was known as the Pellings and were said to be respected in Wales. One was Thomas Rowlands, the father of Lady Bukeley. They claimed descent from a young man who had married a fairy he caught near a lake. The fairy's name is given as Penelope. She only married him on condition he would not touch her with iron, but he did so accidentally. She may have come from Cwellyn Lake, because it was near where he caught her. One version of the tale says she was not allowed to return to him, but could talk to him from a floating island in the lake. *Penelope* was not, I suspect, the original name of the fairy.

It was said that at Llyn Cwm Lwch there was a cave in the mountains. Once a year a door in the cave was left open. This enabled people to enter a passage which led to an island in the middle of the lake – a fairy realm. However, a man tried to take flowers from the islands, whose tenants reduced him to idiocy, while the door never appeared again in the cave. While this is merely a legend, it does show that in

Wales it was a very definite idea that access to the fairy realm could be obtained through lakes and that the fairies did not necessarily live in the lake itself, but in a place which could be reached by way of a lake. The fairy island could not be seen clearly from the lakeshore, but a vague visual complication could be discerned by the onlooker.

In Derbyshire there are two lakes which are supposed to contain mermaids. If you see the mermaid at Mermaid's Pool, you will gain immortality. On the other hand, at Black Mere in Morridge Moor, there is a mermaid who will pull you into the water. Be sure not to mix them up.

In a small lake on the Isle of Skye the *luideag*, a ferocious demoness, is said to dwell. Another spirit better avoided was the English *Jenny Greenteeth* who had green teeth and hair and was very thin and would pull children into the water. The name was also applied to duckweed, which looks deceptively like firm ground until you step on it, when you sink. It is probable that Jenny Greenteeth was invented to keep children away from the waterside. Jenny Greenteeth was sometimes to be found in trees. In the east of Europe, the *rusalka* performs a similar function. She is very beautiful with green hair. Some say the *vodyany*, a male spirit, controls rusalkas. He too lives in the river and, if you fall in and drown, he will feast on your body and place your soul in a jar.

The ancient Greeks believed in sea-nymphs called *Nereids*. These were the offspring of the sea-divinities Nereus and Doris. Prominent among them were Amphitrite, wife of Poseidon, the chief sea god, and Thetis, the mother of Achilles. In modern Greece the term nereid is used for a wide variety of nymphs and fairies. Nereids are sometimes said to interbreed with humans, but the offspring of such unions are often nasty.

A couple of modern encounters were related to R. and E. Blum. A soldier claimed he was pelted with pebbles by a nereid when he tried to drink from a river. Another witness passing a pond also had pebbles thrown at him. Then he saw a nereid playing a mandolin. Afterwards, many nereids emerged from the pond and headed for the seashore. The folklorist Lawson said he had met a man who claimed his grandmother had been a nereid. His fellow villagers backed him up in this story. In fact, amorous encounters between humans and nereids seem to be the subject of quite widespread belief. Authoress Dorothy Ratcliffe was told of a man who had an amorous encounter with a nereid, but lost his sanity. Authoress Dorothy Lee met a man who claimed his father-in-law had surprised nereids trying to steal

a baby at night. The cock crew and the nereids dropped the baby
and ran. The Greeks believed in another kind of mermaid called the
Gorgona or *Phokia* who was to be found in stormy waters.

The term for a Germanic river merman is *nix*. (Sometimes in
English *neck* is used). The female is a *nixe*. In Sweden he can be known
as a *Strömkarl*, in Norway as a *Fossegrim*. Some were regarded as luring
women and children into the water with their violin playing. Some
were shape shifters. The most famous German river mermaid *Lorelei*
is not a genuine folklore personage at all: she was invented by Clemens
Brentano in *Zur Bacharach im Rhein* (1801) and subsequently became
the heroine of Heine's celebrated poem *Die Lorelei* (1821).

The River Elbe is said to be the chief location of the *alven*, also
called the *ottermaaner*. They enter bubbles to enable themselves to fly,
as they are wingless. They dress in otter skins.

In Catalunya the water-fairies, although they are not exclusively
found near water, are called *dones d'agua*. They look like beautiful
women, but are sometimes half fish or half bird.

Turning to Arthurian romance, lakes seem to be associated with
the Otherworld. Thus the magic sword Excalibur is obtained from and
returned to the Lady of the Lake. Lancelot was raised by a lake fairy. In
stories of persons who have married lake fairies, their home is under
the waters. The story of Lancelot and Guinevere descends from French
romance, but a very different one about Lancelot comes from Ulrich
von Zatzikhoven, a German writer, in his *Lanzelet*. His work seems to
be based on the original story, because it contains Celtic elements. For
example, the son of the Lady of the Lake is called *Mabuz*, whom in
Welsh we find as *Mabon*. He is a cymrified version of *Maponos* son of
the goddess *Matrona,* the original of Morgan La Fée, whose dwelling
place was in the Otherworld of Avalon. We cannot help wondering if,
in the original versions of these stories, the lake was seen, not as where
the fairies lived, but as a passage to where the fairies dwelt – to use
modern parlance, a sort of wormhole leading to the Otherworld.

A scary story set in modern Somerset is told by folklorist Jon
Dathen. His informant Jenny was a horsewoman. Once when she was
out on her horse she entered some woodland. They approached a small
lake. The horse seemed nervous. Looking into the water, Jenny saw a
naked white woman with dirty golden long hair beneath the surface.
She smiled at Jenny who felt cold and seemed unable to move, but felt
she had to. She also had a compulsion to go into the water, but felt that
would spell her doom. The woman, who never rose out of the water,

made what looked like a beckoning gesture. Jenny pulled herself away and made off as quickly as possible.

Finally, let us turn our attention to a creature reported in modern times, what may be called a mer-being, in the Caspian Sea, which, as the reader may know, is the world's largest lake. It 2005 an Iranian newspaper, the *Zingadi*, carried a very strange report. An Azerbaijani ship, the *Baky*, observed what they at first took to be a fish in its waters. Then they saw it was no fish they had ever seen. It had hairs on its head; it had arms; it had four webbed fingers on each hand; its feet were seal-like; it had scales on the tip of its nose, looking like a dolphin's beak; its stomach was rough-edged. The *Zingadi* started to receive many letters from people claiming to have seen the creature. It was called in Farsi *Runan Shah* (water king). It has been suggested it had lived in the deeper part of the lake, but had been forced up by volcanic activity. It was suspected that there was more than one of them and that they were making inroads on the lake's supply of sturgeon.

With regard to the possible relationship of mermaids to humans, various sources on the Internet assure me that humans do not have the correct DNA to produce gills; yet Benwell and Waugh assert that some babies are born with vestigial gills which they sometimes have to have surgically removed. They even claim to have heard of a woman born with a complete set of gills.

Mermaids are, of course, not the only strange creatures reported from the sea. In a television show of 1991, the actress Shelley Winters said that, during the course of World War II, when she was on the Pacific coast, a creature that she at first mistook for a frogman emerged from the water. It was, in fact, a red humanoid that hugged her with both hands. In 1989 a man named Shane in Australia saw, by the sea, a humanoid creature about 6' tall covered with green scales. His hands and feet were webbed. He had a fin which stretched from the centre of his forehead down his back. Also, he had fins going from wrist to waistline. Shane felt he received a telepathic message from the being telling him not to be afraid.[33]

---

33 M. Smith *Bigfoots and Bunyips* (Alexandria, NSW, 1996), pp. 185-6

Chapter Eight
fairy artefacts

I F there is any reality behind the stories of Fairies, it is likely that some traces of them are to be found in things they have allegedly wrought. It has been said erroneously that nothing supposed to have been made by the fairies has been found. But the Fairy Flag of Dunvegan is an example of such an object. It is perhaps the most famous artefact attributed to a fairy origin.

The Fairy Flag is to be seen today at Dunvegan Castle on the Isle of Skye in Scotland. It is made of silk. The story is that a chief of the Clan MacLeod – some say Iain Ciar or his father Malcolm – encountered a fairy and they fell in love. The fairy's father, a king, said they could not marry, but then relented, saying they could marry for a year and a day or, in another version, for twenty years. In the latter version the Fairy Bride left her husband at the Fairy Bridge, as she flew away, dropping the flag.

In the other version, they had a son. When the Fairy left, she begged her grief-stricken husband to ensure the baby was never left alone. The husband was plunged into melancholia, so his clansmen held a party to cheer him up. The baby's nurse went down to the party. When the Chief realised his son was alone, he rushed to his room. There he saw the Fairy leaning over the cradle, but she vanished on his appearance. He discovered she had wrapped the baby in the Fairy Flag. In another version, the nurse was bidden to bring the baby down and found that fairies had wrapped him in the flag. When she appeared with him, a fairy chorus began to sing, saying the Flag could save the baby three times.

A different version says a MacLeod returning from Crusade confronted a demoness called Nein a Phaipen. They fought and he defeated her. She gave him her girdle, which became the Flag. A variant is that he obtained the Flag from a Fairy on the way home.

Sir Walter Scott, writing of the Flag, said it had three powers: to increase the number of men in the host on a battlefield; to induce fertility; and to bring herring into the loch.

An argument has been put forward that it is in fact the Landoda, a flag brought from the Middle East by King Harald III of Norway, which eventually came into the hands of the MacLeods.

When a fire broke out in the castle in 1938, the Flag was carried past it and it went out.

Because of the many stories about the Flag's source, it cannot be said with certainty to be of fairy origin, though, if it was really responsible for extinguishing the flames in 1938, it does show some preternatural power.

Another such famous relic is the Luck of Edenhall. It is a drinking glass, flared at the top, decorated with enamel and gilding. This is said to have been found by a servant of the Musgrave family of Edenhall in Cumbria when fairies were dancing around it. He picked it up and took it with him. The fairies said that if it broke or fell, the luck of Edenhall would depart with it. Received wisdom would place its origin in the Near East in the 14th Century. It is first referred to in writing as the Luck of Edenhall in 1677. It was lent to the Victoria and Albert Museum in 1926 and permanently acquired by it in 1958.

Again, one can hardly infer from this artefact that it is proof of the fairy manufacture to which it is ascribed. The legend of the Musgrave servant may have grown up because of the manufacture of the vessel, which could not have been duplicated in England until much later than that time. Once again we do not have anything sufficient to prove absolutely the existence of fairies here.

If these two famous alleged fairy artefacts cannot be regarded as proof positive of the existence of fairies, let us turn to humbler objects. In 1835 a shoe, dubbed the Fairy Shoe, was found in Ireland by a farmer. It was less than 3" long and 1" at its broadest part. It was in due course examined by Harvard scientists who said the stitching, though tiny, was done by hand. Nor is this the only such shoe discovered. Did tiny people make the tiny shoes and, if not, why were they made and by whom?[34]

A tiny fully lined coat was discovered (location not specified) in 1868. It had cloth covered buttons and showed much signs of wear.[35]

Michael O'Shea in 1972 discovered a tiny waistcoat (in American English=vest) with a single silver button and tiny breeches. Clothing such as this is not that unusual in Ireland.

Tiny pipes are also well-known. In Wales small pipes with tiny bowls, called *cefyn y Tylwyth Teg* (fairy pipes) turn up from time to

---

34 gummerfansmonsterhunting.blogspot.com
35 *Ib.*

time. They often have the stems broken off, but the bowls are intact.[36] In England, Scotland and Ireland, tiny pipes are called fairy pipes and even, in England, Mab's pipes after the queen of the fairies.[37] A little clay pipe was found before 1893 in a field at Kettleshulme (Cheshire). The tobacco in it was still lit, indicating it had been in use only shortly before. It is unlikely to have been a salesman's sample.

If these pipes antedate the introduction of tobacco, we must ask what the fairies, or whoever smoked them, were smoking. The answer would seem to be herbs of some sort. Humans actually smoked local herbs before tobacco was introduced from America.

There are many so-called fairy houses on the Isle of Skye. However, they may have been occupied by a short race of ordinary humans. Sir Iain Noble of Hotel Eilean Iarman says there have been records of conversations between people and fairies.

At Beetham in Cumbria there is a miniature flight of steps, too small for human use. Local opinion has it they were made by and for fairies.

Flint arrowheads, sometimes known as *elf-shot*, were considered to be fairy artefacts. They were said to transfer diseases to cattle, horses and people. However, any archaeologist will assign them to our human ancestors.

A dwarf king named Goldemar or Vollmar left some artefacts behind him, though we have no reason to think he made them himself. He had taken up residence in Hardenstein Castle in the Ruhr and, though people never saw him, he allowed himself to be touched. He was a virtuoso on the harp, with which he enchanted his listeners. Once, someone strewed ashes and tares in his way, hoping he would fall over so his footprints might be seen. This unhappy ash strewer, however, was unaware that Goldemar was coming up behind him. He cut him into pieces and placed his body on a spit for roasting purposes. He boiled the head and legs and retired to his room, where he consumed them. The roast meat and spit remained in the castle until they disappeared in wartime in 1651. When Keightley wrote his *Fairy Mythology* (1850) the pot was still there, built into the wall of the kitchen.

None of this comes into the category of conclusive proof of fairies' existence. However, it rebuts the claim that nothing which could ever be termed a fairy artefact has been found and that's why this chapter has been included here.

---

36 www.welsh-mythsandlegends.walesdirectory.co.uk
37 E.R. Billings *Tobacco* (Teddington, n.d.), p. 139

Chapter Nine

the giant and his kin

PERHAPS the most terrifying character of fairytale is the giant. He is so huge that his very size makes you want to be elsewhere. He is bestial, wishing only to devour his victims. Jehovah's Witnesses and Mormon missionaries call at his castle door at their peril. He is often so stupid that it is quite impossible to reason or negotiate with him. The only hope of the possible victim is to outsmart him. In pictorial representations he often carries a club, implying that his mental limitations preclude his manufacturing more sophisticated weaponry.

Belief in giants is widespread. The Greeks regarded the Giants as the sons of Uranus and Gaea, who launched an attack on Olympus but were driven off. Modern Greek giants are sometimes called *drakoi*. They are not very bright and sometimes eat humans. Another type of Greek giant is called the *arapis* and is black. It sometimes smokes a long pipe. The Germanic giants seem to have been considered the same size as gods, for they intermarried. In Norse they were called *iotunn* from a Proto-Germanic **itunoz*, which in turn seems to be the origin of Scots *etin*. Giants also figured among the Slavs and sundry other peoples. Therefore we will now try to look into what the origin of belief in giants may be.

When primitive people saw structures that they could not believe had been made by humans of ordinary size, they sometimes ascribed them to giants. Thus Stonehenge was formerly called the Giants' Dance. Roads composed of blocks of stone seemingly too heavy to lift were ascribed to giants. The Giant's Causeway in Ireland was also ascribed to a giant, no less than Finn mac Cool (Irish: *Fionn mac Cumhaill*) who was in origin a god. His gigantic stature was a later attribute.

It has been suggested that giants were the gods of primitive peoples who, yielding to the mythologies of more sophisticated later races, consigned them to a primitive existence. Ymir, a huge giant, was the father of the Norse gods Odin, Vili and Ve, who were worshipped in historical times by the Norse. One wonders, however, if a giant god like Ymir was the deity of the pre-Norse inhabitants of Scandinavia, displaced by incoming Norse gods. Odin himself seems to have displaced Tyr as the chief of the gods. Grimm suggests *iotunn* may have come from the name of those who inhabited Jutland before the influx of the historical Jutes. C. von Sydow has suggested that giants were folklore figures invented to explain natural phenomena or large structures, only later entering into mythology.

The Celts had two mighty giants, each with a single eye that shot out a deadly beam. Amongst the Irish there was Balor, while the Welsh had Yspaddaden Penkawr. These were almost certainly sun-gods demoted to the rank of giants once they ceased to be worshipped in the Christian era. The clue is in the single powerful eye. The same, of course, may have happened to other ex-gods. For example, one author argues that the legendary giant Tom Hickathrift may have been a god of the Iceni, in the area of which ancient tribe he was supposed to have flourished. On the other hand, very tall men may have become giants in folk belief. The Herefordshire giant Jack o' Legs was said to be able to look into people's upstairs windows, yet it is quite possible he was in origin a very tall man. Such a man can be transformed easily into a giant.

The Bulgarians gave an interesting attribute to their giants. They were vulnerable to blackberry bushes and, as their eyes were so high above the bushes, they often didn't see them and stumbled into them.

In the far off Philippines, they believe in a hairy giant called the *kapre* (also spelled *capre*) that wears a loincloth and smokes a pipe or cigar. If you take its white stone, it will grant wishes. Sightings of this creature are said to be not uncommon in Southern Leyte. There are also reports of sightings in Luzon, while a sighting is said to have occurred in Cebu in 1985.

While all the above factors may have given rise to the concept of the giant, yet I feel there may be something more tangible behind it also, but, before we approach that, I should like to turn my attention to the *ogre* of fairytale.

The ogre would seem to go back to Orcus, an Italian god of the Underworld. It later became *orco/huorco* as a common noun. In the Tyrol you find *orke, lorke* used for a Wildman. The reason I include it with giants is because ogres are sometimes, but not always, giants. They have a generally humanoid appearance and an appetite for human flesh, which I understand is thought to taste like pork, though I have never sampled it. I suspect that, apart from the origins assigned to the giants above, there is another origin which can also be assigned to the ogre.

Both giants and ogres and sometimes also trolls are connected with another creature of folklore, the Wildman. This creature was supposed to be a large hairy human or subhuman that dwelt in forest and fell. He was often larger than the average man and regarded as dangerous. Such creatures are still reported in America (as *bigfoot/sasquatch*), in Guatemala (as *sisemite*), in China (as *xing-xing*) and in numerous other places, especially in the Himalayas as the Abominable Snowman (which may include more than a single species). Of course, although these creatures are reported, this does not mean they actually exist – but they could. However, such creatures have also been reported from Europe, some comparatively recently, and encounters with them could certainly have given rise to tales of Giant and Ogre. In addition, people sometimes dressed in Wildman costumes at festivals, which should have etched the image clearly into people's consciousness.

In England itself, the Wildman was called the Wodewose. However, it is doubtful that such beings ranged the English forests. Nonetheless, the Continent is another matter. Tales of the wodewose may have been brought to England by invading Anglo-Saxons and Norsemen. The Germans called such creatures *Waltmann* and *Waltuodor*. The female of the species they referred to as a *Wild Wip*. Among the Basques there are references to *Basa Jaun*, sometimes an individual, sometimes a species, though only about human size. The *Getzko* is the Wildman of Poland. The Komi of European Russia believed in the *Yagmort*. Certainly, breeding populations of such creatures could have once existed in Europe. Reports even continue up to today.

In 1407, James Egelinus, Scottish mariner, was wrecked on the Norwegian coast. There he saw wildmen and was told by the locals that they would attack human households and make a meal of their inhabitants. These may have been trolls. In France in 1646, two wildmen were supposedly encountered by loggers. In 1661 a "bearman" was captured in Lithuania. In the same century a wildman was captured in Poland. Wild women were reported in Brandenburg in 1735. A Wildman was reported in the Pyrenees in 1774. In the same century a Wildman was captured in Kronstadt (Russia).

Writing in 1850, Benjamin Thorpe suggested there were actually primitive people living in Sweden who gave rise to such stories. He suggested this because there were so many stories of trolls told by credible people. In Croatia there were wildmen called *vedi* who were hair-covered and tall, said to be taller than houses, though this may be an exaggeration and anyway houses were not very big in the old days in Croatia. They perhaps existed until the 20th Century and there may even be still a few about. They had woodland settlements and wore ragged clothes. Some would capture humans and keep them as slaves, but eventually let them go. Some actually attached themselves to human homes. The Croatians also believed in *shumske dekle* (woodland girls) who were naked but hair-covered (though less so on the faces). Intellectually they were inferior to humans. It seems to the present writer possible they were the females of the *vedi*, as they were found in the same regions. In Slovenia there were wildmen called *divji noz*, forest-dwellers generally friendly to humans. The French in the Alps region called Wildmen *Sarradons* and in 1958 a local told folklorists his mother had seen them. They used to come into Saint-Maximin to beg, so not all of them can have been man-eating terrors. In Germany tracks which resembled those of humans' were found as recently as 1970 and a humanoid creature was seen near Hahn in 1985. One was reported in Sweden in the same year. Somewhat earlier, A. Couloris reported giant humanoids in Greece in 1978. Two men claimed they were attacked by Wildmen in Spain in 1993.

Italian wildmen were reported from both Alps and Appenines. Although of solitary bent, it is said they were once not uncommon. There are modern reports from 1974, 1980 and 1997.

Recently Nick Redfern has produced a book on wildmen in Britain. Britain could not have sustained a population of wildmen over the centuries unnoticed by the populace. The suggestion has been made that they live underground, but this seems unlikely. An alternative explanation for sightings of such creatures will be found later in this work.

Trolls have long been the subject of belief in Scandinavia, but the term has been applied to different creatures. The term is applied to diminutive or human sized beings that come out in the daytime. There are medium sized trolls, generally caudate, that are hairy and are the size of a human or larger. The third category is of gargantuan proportions and seems to sport extra heads or limbs betimes. Giant trolls, if they outstay the night and are struck by the rays of the sun, will turn into rocks in Norway and trees in Sweden.

It seems we may well find the explanation for the widespread belief in giants in Europe could stem from humanoids as yet unrecognised by zoology, combined with speculation as to how natural features arose or how certain human structures were erected. It is perhaps surprising that Paracelsus, in the 16th Century, apparently felt sexual encounters between humans and wild women were not uncommon. This may have been the result of too much inbreeding among the humanoids.

The major objection to the existence of wildmen in Europe is the lack of remains. Certainly Neanderthals and modern humans co-existed for a time and even interbred and they may have given rise to some stories of ogres, but gigantic humans seem to be another question altogether. Neanderthals were in fact a little smaller than humans. Their predecessor, *Homo heidelbergensis*, was not a gigantic creature, but may have been noticeably larger than early *Homo sapiens*. Belief by humans was possibly kindled by the discovery of the bones of prehistoric animals. The plains of Thessaly, where the battle of gods and giants in Greek mythology was supposed to have taken place, certainly had such bones. However, the widespread belief in giants of superhuman size may have had something more tangible behind it. It may consist in the fact that *Homo sapiens* once co-existed with other humanoid species and the memory and perhaps even in some remote places the species has remained. These could certainly account for reports of wildmen and a Wildman could grow into a giant in popular story with the passage of time, especially if they were burlier and sturdier than humans.

Apart from this, there have been many reports of the unearthing of gigantic human remains in sundry parts of the world, but these remains show a habit of disappearing suggestive of hoaxing. However, should the reader be interested, lists are provided in the superb cryptozoology works of Eberhart and Newton. I will draw the reader's attention to a couple. In 1890 G. Vacher de la Page in Castelnau-de-Lace, France, discovered huge human bones in a cemetery. Their owner is estimated to have been 11.5'/3.5m tall. P.L.A. Kiener (Montpelier School of Medicine) said they represented a very large race. More recently, a human skeleton 8'-10' was supposedly found in the Caucasus in Georgia.

While in the region of the Caucasus, there is a belief in a kind of Wildman there called the *almas*. One of these was actually captured in the 19th Century and kept at Tkhina, a village in Abkhazia. At first she was very wild, but in due course she became tamer and was allowed to wander freely round the village. Her skin was black or dark grey, her body was covered with reddish black hair. She never learned to talk, her facial expression was entirely animal, her face was terrifying and she had large teeth. She never slept indoors and she never learned to speak. A person or persons in the village made her pregnant. When the first two children were born to her, she tried to wash them in the river, but, being half-breeds, they could not stand the cold and perished. One infers that, whatever creature Zana was, such lustrations were usual among them. However, later children that she had were saved by the villagers. They grew up human in their outlook, but they had some unusual physical and mental traits. One of them, Kwit, died in 1954. Russian scientists have examined his skull and their opinion seemed to be he had no Neanderthal traits. Recently, Dr Bryan Sykes (Oxford University) has done DNA tests on Zana's descendants. These reveal she was human and of sub-Saharan African ancestry. She may have been descended from a primitive African population that entered Asia millennia ago and left descendants, of whom Zana was one. It is also possible other descendants of this group ventured elsewhere in Europe, explaining the Wildman legend to an extent, if they lived into historical times.

Giant humans were supposed to live in Patagonia, Argentina. Pigafetta, who accompanied Magellan, said that in 1520 he had seen a man double the normal size. Various reports came in over the centuries, some of them speaking of men 12' tall. A. Guyat was unsuccessful in an attempt to bring some to France in 1766. Perhaps some of these estimates were due to exaggeration, but it may be that a very tall tribe once dwelt there, but intermarried with others, leading to a reduction in height.

Mark A. Hall and Loren Coleman harbour a different theory about giants. They have put forward a theory that giants are the descendants of Gigantopithecus, remembered by humans. The fossil record for Gigantopithecus ends no later than 300,000 years ago, but that doesn't necessarily mean that Gigantopithecus ceased to exist at that time. Gigantopithecus has been considered by zoologists to have been a huge ape, but Hall and Coleman believe it was a hominid (*Giganthropus*). Its height and nature have been inferred from four huge jawbones and about 1000 teeth. These have been found only in India, China and Vietnam. It is possible Gigantopithecoi crossed the Bering Strait into the Americas and also managed the trip overland as far as Europe, but no remains indicating their presence have come to light.

However, many reports of gigantic hominids have come in from sundry parts of the world and these reports suggest the existence of a creature considerably larger than the Bigfoot of North America. These creatures are slim, hair-covered and sport flat faces. It is said they wield clubs, eat humans and live in secret caves. These are, suggest Hall and Coleman, descendants of Gigantopithecus and are 10'-12' tall. This should mean they are pretty noticeable. Despite the fact that the remains of their ancestors come from eastern Asia, Hall and Coleman feel they are now found worldwide.

What might count as a giant is the legendary *Orang Gadang* of Sumatra and Borneo. This is rumoured to exist on those islands and its existence has never been disproved. It may be a large ape and it is said to attain a height of 10 feet. However, though it sports luxuriant head hair, the hair on its body is sparse.

Modern reports of such giants are not unknown. For example, Zollie Owens at Hallsville (Texas) claimed to have seen a 12' giant in 1976.

Barry Chemish seems to feel giants are turning up in Israel at the present time. On April 20th, 1993, Tsiporet Carmel saw a being 7' in height in Kadima. It seemed to be standing near a self-constructing silo. In July of the same year two 7' tall bald creatures appeared on the seventh floor apartment of Batya Shimon in Rishan Letzin. In December in a village called Yatzitz, Danny Ezra opened a door to see a 9' creature whose face was concealed by a haze. Further giant sightings have been reported. Chamish seems to think these giants have come out of UFOs.

A modern account of a giant sighting in Pennsylvania was passed on to paranormal researcher Stan Gordon. The witness claimed the incident took place on 18th March, 2011. At night time he saw a gigantic figure cross the road in front of him. His skin, which seemed to be of a brown colouration, was smooth, like leather. There was a ridge on the top of its head.

M. Boirayon has argued that there is a population of giants in the Solomon Islands. He feels that the population of giants on Guadalcanal numbers hundreds or perhaps even thousands. There are also populations on other islands. He asserts that on Tangarare there are humans of giant descent, the result of hybridisation. He tells us that giants once ate people, but have thoughtfully discontinued the practice. They are also said to have a form of writing. It is said Ezekiel Alebua, who was Prime Minister of the Solomon Islands 1986-9, was, as a boy, shown a 15' skeleton.

In days agone (but I have been unable to discover how far agone) wildmen were said to be found at Yellowham Hill in Dorset.

At this juncture I might mention that in parts of Africa people fear attack by human-gorilla hybrids. Apparently the fathers of these ogres (for I think we may call them that) were human, but, encountering female gorillas, they mistook them for beautiful women. The result was the hybrids. It surely dawns upon the reader that the fathers of these creatures would have been visually challenged. Strong spectacles were obviously lacking here. We might also mention that, amongst the Sudanese, hunters are supposed to mate sometimes with lionesses. I would strongly suggest that you do not try this yourself, as the attempt is likely to be unsuccessful and the outcome painful. The result of some such unions are said to be beautiful daughters, but, if you marry one, she may eat you. Don't say you haven't been warned.

Legends regarding giants were doubtless reinforced in the public mind by figures of giants kept in certain cities. These include:

London: Gog and Magog
Douai: Gayant
Brussels: a family of giants
Louvain: Hercules and Megara
Lille: Lyderic and Phinart
Antwerp: Antigonus

Chapter Ten

goatmen

tHE idea that reports have come in of creatures that look like men as far down as the waist and having the legs of a goat below that will astonish many a reader, yet this is in fact the case. Before we start taking a look at modern reports, however, we shall take a view at their ancient antecedents.

First of all, we can discount the Greek *satyr* from our consideration, for satyrs were originally depicted with parts not of a goat, but with horses' legs and ass's ears. Later, however, they became to some extent confused with the Roman *fauns* and were depicted as part man and part goat. Apart from Greece, they were said to live in North Africa.

The most famous goat-god in Greek mythology was, of course, *Pan*, who was normally depicted as human above the waist with horns and a beard, while below the waist he resembled a goat. He was to be found in rustic and bosky places and invented the pan-pipes. His shout caused those who heard it to panic. He may have been a pre-Hellenic god, in that he does not really fit well into the structure of Greek myth. He is supposed to have had various different parents, which may mean that, in the original myths told of him, none were known. Arcadia, a backward country area which was rather disdained, was the centre of his cult and was just the place where belief in a pre-Hellenic deity might survive. The first time we find a mention of Pan is in the works of Pindar (*fl.* 5th Century BC), though one suspects his cultus goes back a great deal further.

Pan was one of a species. There were a whole tribe of goatmen supposedly living in ancient Greece. In English, they are referred to as *pans* and they sometimes had the heads as well as the legs of goats.

In the myths of Rome there were half-men, half-goat sprites called *fauns*, which were male and female. There was also an individual god called Faunus who had a wife called Fauna. The ancient Italians, too, then, believed in goatmen. The belief persisted into recent times. In modern Italy the child of fauns is called an *incubus*. This was a creature that gave bad dreams to the animals – his very name indicates a nightmare. The exact relationship of this to the sexual incubus who assaults women by night may be seen from reading a later chapter.

So we have traditions of goatmen in both Greece and Italy. In Scotland, also, there is a small goat-sprite called a *urisk* which does housework in the Highlands, just as the brownie does in the Lowlands. Danish folklore features the *geteman*, which will jump out of a bush and scare you. German forests are said to be the haunt of the *bockmann*. In the Czech Republic they had the *chatez*. But the notion of goat-beings seems so preposterous that we should dismiss it altogether, were it not for the fact that reports of goatmen are coming in even today.

The most famous modern Goatman is perhaps that of Prince George's County (Maryland). It is described as covered in dark hair, with a human's upper body and a goat's legs. It was first seen in 1957. Sundry reports came in of the strange creature. For a time, the Goatman seems to have disappeared and was seen no more until 1967. It was also reported in 1971 and 1973. The last report seems to have been around 1985.

Could such a creature, part man and part goat, represent a kind of strange species in the Maryland countryside? If so, it may be very dangerous, as it is said to harbour an aversion to humans and to wield an axe. Some say the goatman may be a solitary creature, the result of a scientific experiment that went wrong. The presence of the nearby National Agricultural Research Center has fuelled such an idea. But this Goatman is not the only one, as we shall see.

In Tarrant County, Texas, is Lake Worth, where another goatman is said to reside. The first reports concerning it came in in 1969. It was said to be half man and half goat. It was observed by John Reichart and his wife and two other couples, when it came crashing out of a tree. It seemed to be covered in scales and fur. It banged into the Reicharts' car, then ran off. On reporting this to the police, the Reicharts discovered the creature was already under police investigation, as there had been previous reports. The next night it was seen crossing the road near the Lake Worth Nature Center.

One problem is that the creature was sometimes described as dark, sometimes white. Was there more than one creature? Was the whole thing no more than a hoax, with perpetrators wearing different costumes?

Some time later, a group saw and pursued the creature, but, as they approached him, he flung a large tyre at them. Their collective nerve broke and they scattered.

Connected to the lakeside by what Tennyson would have called a dark strait of barren land (though perhaps it isn't barren – I haven't been there) is Greer Island and it is suspected the creature lived there. Allan Plaster, dress shop proprietor, took a photograph of a great white beast with a very small head. Was this the same creature the others had seen? Reports continued.

The years passed, but in 2005 Nick Redfern, Ken Gerhart and his wife Lori decided to go to Greer Island and have a look around. They saw no goatman, but did feel they were being watched. They also found a curious structure made of wood. Such structures are often found in vicinities where Bigfoots are said to be found. It looked a little like a pyramid, fashioned out of branches torn from trees. They found an area of flattened ground where they surmised some creature had been sitting and the remains of a fish it had been devouring.

There was a caravan site nearby and Nick has suggested the Goatman was a child deformed by inbreeding, as it seems to be a common belief in America that those who live on caravan sites (called in the United States trailer parks) often find inbreeding a congenial pastime. While it may well happen, it doesn't automatically follow that wherever you find a trailer park, such activity necessarily takes place.

Redfern lived in Dallas, Texas, for a time and near Dallas is White Rock Lake. This is a body of water to which legends tend to accrue. A goatman is said to live in this region as well. There have been various stories about it. In 2001, Sandy Grace was jogging around the lake when she encountered this figure. It was covered in brown hair and appeared to have horns. It vanished in a flash of light. The description provided does not say if it had caprine hooves.

Let us now travel north to Vermont. There, in the 1960s, a goatman was reported in Jericho. Though reports seem to have ceased, there is the idea that it may have hied itself to Mount Mansfield and may flourish there even today. This goatman had shown a tendency to look through people's windows, which they must have found startling.

In Utica (Nebraska) a goatman was reported in 1982. Ten years earlier, one had been reported in Marshall (Texas). Another Texan goatman is associated with Old Alton Bridge, Denton. At South Mills (Kentucky) there were reports of one in the 1970s. There seem to be some traditions of such a creature at Burnt Mountain (Georgia), but I could unearth little information about this.

Goatwomen are less regularly reported. The *glaistig* of Scotland is sometimes described as half woman, half goat, but the term seems to be rather loosely applied. In Italy, in the region of Cadore, tradition exists of the beautiful *longana*, who is half goat. The Argentine newspaper *La Razon* reported a goatwoman at Limonas, Peru, in 1972.

It is perhaps surprising that these sundry descriptions of goatmen tend to exist on the American continent in modern times, while in ancient times they were features of Mediterranean culture. What inference we might draw from this, I cannot say.

I will spare a moment here to look at the curious narrative of R. Ogilvie Crombie. This worthy claimed to have seen a faun in the Royal Botanic Gardens in Edinburgh and later to have met Pan himself, who declared himself a servant of God. Crombie, in describing the sighting of the faun, said he was not using his ordinary sight to see him. Yet he seemed sure the experience was not imaginary. He brought the faun home and showed him the inside of his house.

The fact that Crombie was not using his normal sight, as he freely admits, leads me to suspect that the encounter was, in fact, hallucinatory. However, I cannot rule out the possibility that there is some alternative form of visual apprehension that he might have employed.

Keeping to the mythical creatures of the ancients, what about centaurs? Incredible as it seems, there are two reports of sightings of centaurs in modern times. In 1963 James McKinney of Centerville (Illinois) rang the police to report a centaur. Another was later reported from Melbourne (Florida).[38] It had been my understanding that centaurs were a physiologically impossible kind of creature – but maybe they are not as physiologically impossible as hitherto supposed. The Centaurs of Greek legend may preserve the memory of a tribe who brought horses into Greece for the first time. The are generally depicted as uncouth, though one of them, Chiron, was regarded as a wise tutor of heroes.

In the legends of the Poncan Indians of Nebraska, there was a woman with the legs and hooves of a deer. A dangerous creature, she obviously didn't like men, whom she had a tendency to kill. However, you will be relieved to learn that I have received no accounts of sightings of this fearsome creature.

Other such creatures with the features of man and beast seem to inhabit lakes. Thus lakes in Montana were said to be home to the

---

38 B.M. Nunnelly *The Inhumanoids* (Woolfardisworthy, 2011), pp.201-2. My own
     investigations suggest there may have been other witnesses to the Centerville
     centaur.

Beaver Women. These had beaver like fur on their legs and backs and would lure men into the water, but what happened to them then is anybody's guess, for there is no record of their emergence. The Beaver Women would steal girls and boys, the girls later becoming Beaver Women themselves, the boys being murdered. The Great Lakes of North America were supposedly occupied by the Serpent Woman, who was a hundred feet long. Her upper body was human, but was covered with silver scales. The lower body was that of a serpent. She had a brace of fangs which protruded from her mouth and claws instead of fingernails. She lured men into the water to be her lovers, but they would soon change into monsters themselves.

Bird Women are a race of beautiful winged women said to dwell in the Rocky Mountains.[39]

While the Goatmen seem to have an existence, the other creatures mentioned in this chapter, in my opinion, represent some kind of fear of women or hatred of men, perhaps at a subconscious level, in the minds of those that invented them. But how could creatures such as Goatmen evolve? Despite eyewitness accounts of their existence, that existence is very hard to explain in terms of our present knowledge.

---

39 W.H. Blackman *The Field Guide to North American Monsters* (New York, 1998), p.100.

Chapter Eleven

the wild hunt

WIDESPREAD in Western Europe we find traditions of the Wild Hunt. So widespread are they, in fact, that I do not purpose to list them all here. I shall merely deal with a number of them and give some explanation of the origin of the belief. Earlier I cited an example from the *Peterborough Chronicle*, but I suggested this was a hoax, performed because certain persons disliked the abbot. However, we cannot be sure of this. The hunt was also reported in Normandy in 1081 by the chronicler Orderic Vitalis. This is earlier than the Peterborough incident.

In northern Germany Woden is often depicted as the leader of the hunt as well he might be, because he is pictured as warlike and furious. He is accompanied by Valkyries and *einheriar* (those who fell in battle). The hunt is sometimes said to include people who died violently before their time. In Sweden Woden, known by his Scandinavian name of Odin, became somewhat demoted with the passage of time and it was said he had been a man who had hunted on Sundays and now was doomed forever. In Smaland, when his hounds grew fatigued, he hunted with birds.

In Westphalia the hunter was called Hackelberand. Again, he went hunting on Sundays and was banished into the air. Sometimes it was said he only hunted from Christmas to Epiphany. It is said that one year one of his hounds was left behind and it stayed waiting for him until he came again a year later.

In Lower Saxony he is called Hans von Hackelberg and he was in charge of the hounds of the Duke of Brunswick. He is supposed to have lived in the 16th Century and his tombstone was shown. Legend has it that he slew a huge boar, which he then kicked. The boar's tusk pierced his foot and mortally wounded him; but he said he didn't wish to go to heaven, but to hunt. When he went hunting through the air, he was preceded by an owl called Tutosel, who had once been a nun. (I do not know if you remain a nun after you have been changed into an owl.) Now it turns out that the term *hakelberand* was once applied to Woden, so I feel we have here Woden under another name. Woden's Wild Hunt may have contributed to the legend of Santa Claus, as he was said to come down through the chimney or a smokehole.

Sometimes the Hunt was led by Frau Goden, a female. She actually seems to have come into existence by a mistake. Someone changed the masculine *fro*, in front of Woden's name, into the feminine *frau*.

It is worth noting, however, that the progresses of the fairies Holda and Berchta were held at about the same time of the year when Hakelberand's Wild Hunt was on the rampage. There can be little doubt that Holda and Berchta were the same goddess in origin. Interestingly, both were at times said to have led the Wild Hunt.

My own opinion had been that the myth of the Wild Hunt had grown from the flight of skeins of geese overhead or the roars of the storm on tempestuous nights. However, the progresses of Holda and Berchta put me in mind of the Roman historian Tacitus, who said the Germans had a goddess called Nerthus, whom they took around the country in a progress on a cart. When the cart arrived at each location, a festival was held. When it wasn't progressing, this cart was kept on an island, possibly at Naerum in Denmark. Often, the progress remained the same in folklore for the females but it was later incorporated into the myth of the wild Odin and given a more furious character. Sometimes, the two myths were melded, making Holda/Berchta into a Wild Huntress. My argument is augmented by the Wild Hunt's being led by a female being in a chariot in Norway. In short, I suspect it was some kind of festival, perhaps held about the time of the winter solstice. It would have involved a procession led by a deity.

I feel the myth of the Wild Hunt then caught on, being brought perhaps to Spain, which was for a time ruled by the Visigoths, to Lombardy by the Lombards and to France by the Franks. The Anglo-Saxons and Danes could have been the ones to introduce it to England, the Norsemen and Normans to have introduced it to Ireland. It is not impossible, however, that I am quite wrong and that this is a primitive legend which overspread the whole of Europe in very early times. Its progress may sometimes have been enacted by maskers, giving rise to the belief in the *callikantzaroi* in Greece. These are supposed to be figures appearing between Christmas and Epiphany, displaying a wide variety of characteristics. They are called *planetaroi* in Cyprus. The original Wild Hunt may have been part of a festival marking the winter solstice.

To list the various persons said to lead the Hunt is not necessary here, but one in particular is to be found in English fairy lore and that is Herne the Hunter, whose connection with the Hunt may be quite artificial.

We first hear of Herne in Shakespeare's *Merry Wives of Windsor*, where we are told:-

> There is an old tale goes that Herne the Hunter,
> Sometime a keeper here in Windsor Forest,
> Doth all the winter time, at still midnight,
> Walk round about an oak with great ragged horns
> And then he blasts the tree and takes the cattle
> And makes milch-kine yield blood and shakes a chain
> In a most hideous and dreadful manner.

This seems to be a description of a ghost. There is no mention of any Wild Hunt here. However W. Harrison Ainsworth in *Windsor Castle* (1843) makes him leader of the Wild Hunt. Whether Ainsworth was using any genuine tradition cannot be determined. In Jutland there was a tradition that the Hunt was led by a Horn Jaeger and Herne is called Horne in an early pirated edition of the play, but these facts are not conclusive evidence of a longstanding Herne legend. However, there have been both sightings and hearings of the Hunt in Windsor Park in modern times.

In 1926 Mrs Walter Legge, JP, member of the Windsor Board of Guardians and Rural District Council heard the baying of hounds outside her house at Windsor. Two years later she and her daughter heard the same thing.

A lady claimed to have seen and heard the hounds in the 1930s, according to a report in the *Slough and Eton Express*, published in 1963. The same paper tells in a report of 1971 that Lord Burton's father claimed to have heard the horn and the braying of Herne's hounds when a boy at Eton.

A man wearing antlers emerged from some undergrowth in the 1920s and was followed by a witness until he came to three oak trees and he walked into one of them. This is recorded in A. Macnaghten, *Haunted Berkshire* (1986). Although this book was published in the 1980s, Macnaghten was born in 1914.

In 1936 two Eton boys claimed to have heard, but not seen, a hunt with hounds.

There is a story that in 1962 two youths in the Great Park found a hunting horn. One blew it. They heard an answering horn. Then they saw a pack of hounds coming towards them and actually saw Herne. They fled.

Another story says that two youths and a teddy-boy were in the park. The teddy boy found a horn and sounded it. They heard the music of hounds approaching them. They fled, but the teddy-boy was struck by an arrow and killed. However, the source of the last tale was Ruth Tongue, whose outpourings should be treated with caution.

In 1976 an unconscious sentry was found at the Castle. He said he had seen one of the statues there grow horns.

What do we make of all this? Is Windsor haunted by a horned huntsman? There seems to be some evidence that this is so. However, bearing in mind the widespread belief in the Wild Hunt on the Continent, is it not possible that witnesses are picking up vague threads of memory that have somehow survived in the area and can occasionally manifest themselves visibly? Has some Wild Hunt procession, perhaps held to mark the winter solstice, left some vague shadow in the atmosphere that can be seen when conditions are right, but is mostly incapable of being descried?

Some have sought to connect Herne with memories of the Celtic horned god. A single inscription discovered in France attests to this god's being called Cernunnos, and the famous Gundestrup Cauldron in Denmark, which was used by Celts but probably made in Thrace, shows a horned figure that may be this god, but might also be a shaman. Is it likely that a tradition of such a god has lingered at Windsor for so long? Who can say?

Could there be some being, who has long haunted the area, who puts in an appearance from time to time and was regarded in more primitive eras as a god? I would not rule that out either.

However, there are parallel legends in Denmark. Thus *Horne-jaeger* hunts female elves in that country, while *Jons-jaeger* rides through the air. King Valdemar IV (reigned 1334-75) is also known to ride from Burre to Gurre.

Chapter Twelve
HOUSEHOLD SPIRITS

OUSEHOLD spirits are those who dwell in a house and look after the family in it. It has been suggested that they look after the family rather than the house and will move when the family moves. *Brownies* are found in the Lowlands of Scotland, the north of England and Northern Ireland. The word in Scottish Gaelic is *bruinidh*, clearly taken from Lowland Scots. When the Peninsular War (1808-16) against the forces of Napoleon in Spain took place, the family brownie of the McKays is said to have accompanied the head of the clan when he went there. If you offer the brownie clothes, he will leave your service. Brownies, though household deities, can live outside the building itself.

Not too different is the *hob*. The *hobthrust* may once have been a distinct outdoor sprite, but the terms are now used interchangeably. One of the Paxton letters written in 1489 refers to *Hob Hynte*, brother of Robin Goodfellow. The word *hob* is thought to be a form of *Robert*. Perhaps these two beings were once identical. It has also been pointed out that the word *hob* was once used to mean a kind of short cape, which these beings may have been conceived as wearing. The *fenodyree* was a helpful sprite on the Isle of Man, but there seems to be some doubt as to whether he was a single being or a species. He would thresh a barnful of corn in a night for those he liked. He was supposed to have a dwelling in Glen Rushen.

In the Highlands the urisk (Scottish Gaelic: *uruisg*), a small being half human and half goat, is the equivalent of the brownie.

In Germany the *kobold* could be a house spirit, although it also was said to be found in mines. Wooden carvings of kobolds seem to have been made with their mouths open, as there was a proverb *to laugh like a kobold*. Kobolds bring good luck to the house if the owner treats them properly. The kobold was often thought to be resident in the hearth, the centre of the home before the television displaced it.

Over in Russia you encounter the *domovoy,* a small hairy man. S. Poberezhny in an Internet article for the Paranormal Research

Society (April 11ᵗʰ, 2011), once found the stovetop in his room turned off and wondered if a domovoy might have been active.

A family which saw a diminutive being in brown clothing with a small hat, 25cm tall, in their home has placed a video on YouTube in which it is described by a ten-year-old boy who claimed to be one of the witnesses. Unfortunately, there is no clue to the place where this occurred. The boy has a North American accent.

A very serious academic work (*Encyclopaedia of Religion and Ethics*) puts forward what I feel to be a decidedly unlikely suggestion for the belief in brownies who did housework by night. The servants, it is postulated, did the work while sleepwalking.

A female brownie named Silkie was said by the two ladies who lived at Denton Hall (Northumbria) about 1939 to be a great help. The house would have been too big for them to manage without her. She even put bunches of flowers on the staircase.[40]

A common *motif* in folklore is for the brownie to leave the family if offered clothing. Something similar occurs in the well-known story of "The Elves and the Shoemaker", when the elves, presented with shoes of their own, depart.

Robin Goodfellow, otherwise known as *Puck,* is perhaps the best known home sprite in English literature, due to his appearance in the works of Shakespeare, Jonson and Kipling. He wasn't entirely a home sprite, but *Robin,* like *hob,* is a shortened form of Robert, and hob denoted such a sprite. Puck may have denoted a species originally, but after Shakespeare it came to be associated with Robin. Robin was both a tricksy spirit and a homesprite rolled into one. Shortly after his appearance in a *A Midsummer Night's Dream* we find him in the poem *The Mad Merry Pranks of Robin Goodfellow,* where we learn he was a son of no less a person than Oberon, King of the Fairies. This poem is, despite its antiquity, both easy to read and easy on the ear. It also tells us how Robin acquired the power to shapeshift. Tom Thumb puts in a cameo appearance, playing on the bagpipes. Robin also appeared in *Love Restored* (1612), a masque by Ben Jonson. However, I have never discovered any sightings. Jacob Grimm suggests he was identical with Robin Hood, but I find this very unlikely. In the Robin Hood ballads, there is no supernatural element at all. The first Robin Hood account which has him involved with magic of which I am aware is Ben Jonson's unfinished play, *The Sad Shepherd.* I include

40 G. Edwards *Hobgoblin and Sweet Puck* (London, 1974)

Robin Goodfellow because of his fame, but not because of his possible existence, yet he represents a fairy type whose existence I would be loathe to dismiss out of hand.

Travelling to the mountainous centre of Europe, we meet in Switzerland another house fairy who rejoices in the name of Jack o' the Bowl.

One of the reasons belief in household spirits is so widespread may stem from ancestor worship, in which an ancestor of the family dwelling in the house was a focus of religious activity. It is even possible that the ancestor in question was buried beneath the house. This would make it a vestige of ancestor worship. I am not sure that I would relish the thought of the spirits of my forebears issuing up through the floorboards as I slept in the night, their ghostly hands attending to sweeping, dusting and plying a vacuum cleaner. Perhaps I am too squeamish.

Chapter Thirteen
fRightening faiRies

NOT all of the fairies were friendly, in fact many of them could be quite frightening at times. They were used to keep children in order, by telling them various spectres would get them if they did not behave. The *bogey* or *bogeyman* posed a threat to those of a difficult disposition, while in America the term *booger* seems now to encompass any kind of frightening creature that cannot be readily identified. For children who found the bogle a bit tame, there was always *Bloody Bones*. Children in Somerset would be told this gruesome being was to be found in some cupboard in the house. He sat there surrounded by the bones of naughty children he had devoured. Children would try to look through the keyhole to see if they could discern this monstrous apparition, but it always seemed too dark in the cupboard. If you used threats like that these days, you would probably be accused of child cruelty and your child put in the charge of a psychologist, but, in an odd way, many children relish gruesome beliefs and stories and one such as this might prove enriching rather than intimidating. Bloody Bones eventually seems to have had his name extended to *Raw-Head-and-Bloody-Bones*, though Raw-Head may originally have been a separate character and he doesn't sound any more pleasant than Bloody Bones. Another Somerset nursery bogle was the *Tankerabogus,* while in nearby Dorset one heard of the dangerous *Spoorn*. On the Isle of Wight, the *Mumpoker* fulfilled the same function. In Germany the *Buseman* was happy to deal with unruly offspring.

These, though, are nursery bogles, used to enforce the iron discipline of days agone. The word bogle itself was used to cover creatures which appeared under different guises. A synonym or near-synonym was boggart. There were some bogles of a very frightening character. Other such dangerous beings were the *bugbear* and the *bull-beggar*. (The latter two may have been thought of originally in the shapes of the animals which form part of their names). The *buggerman* of Maryland may be a relative. The German term was *boggel-mann*.

Among the Austrians, the *tatterman* was a dangerous spirit. Jacob Grimm thought the tatterman might originally have been called the *katterman* and been a cat-headed creature.

The Scots divided the fairies into two sections, the Seelie Court (good) and the Unseelie Court (bad). They also used a Gaelic word *fuath* to mean a spectre generally. This is derived from Old Irish *fuath*, form, shape. In Ireland, the Tuatha Dé Danaan had their foes in the *Fomorians,* whose name possibly indicates 'the subterranean people'. However, some races of fairies featured good and bad alike. Indeed, people were often afraid that the fairy folk would treat them nastily. In writing of what might be termed 'dangerous fairies' we often have to give individual accounts of creatures of an unknown nature.

Take, for example, the Unknown Creature of St Michaels. We can't say much about that, except that it scared those who saw it profoundly, if the account is indeed true. John Stow, the 16th Century chronicler, heard it from his father. Once, when certain men were ringing the bells of St Michaels Church, Cornhill, in London, what was described as "an ugly shape and sight" came in by the south window and alighted on the north. We may infer from this, I think, that whatever it was was flying. All the ringers fell to the floor as if dead. (I have the impression they fainted, but some might have been playing 'possum'.) When they came to, they found what appeared to be claw marks on the north window. Tantalisingly, no one seems to have written down what the creature which made them looked like.

Staying in London, in 1654 a horned humanoid roamed, it was said, around Whitechapel, later to be the scene of the infamous exploits of Jack the Ripper, on Saturday nights. Some people attacked it with weapons, but these just went through it as though it were not there.[41]

In the Midlands of England in the 19th Century, belief in a really strange creature grew up. There seems to have been no description of this being and those who believed in it may not have had any conception of its form. The notion arose among ironworkers that, if they didn't let the fires with which they worked go out from time to time, something strange would come to life in them. What the something strange was is vague, to say the least, but they obviously felt it would harbour unpleasant intentions.

Up in the mountains of Snowdonia in Wales dwells the *Brenin Llwyd* (Grey King), of whom Susan Cooper makes use in one of her novels.

---

41 N. Arnold *Paranormal London*

He was considered the lord of the mist and one might be forgiven for thinking, from early accounts, that he was a personification of the mist itself. However, it has been said there is some kind of animal up there and on one occasion it seems to have attacked a campsite. It was described by one witness as looking somewhat like a bear. It seemed actually to be quite wary of mountaineers.

In Iola (Kansas) in 1903 a most disturbing looking creature was encountered. A man who seems to have been the first to descry it let out a fearful yell and others came running to his aid. They saw there a humanoid creature with horns, long hair and large eyes. I have not been able to discover the outcome of this encounter. The incident is mentioned by Rife.

The next creature may not have been evil at all, but he scared the children who saw him and one of them is said to have described him as "horrid". In January 1967, lightning struck Studham Common where some boys were playing. They saw a little green man about 3' tall, wearing a brimless bowler (American English=derby) hat. He had a flat triangle for a nose. He had a beard. They ran towards him, but he vanished in a puff of smoke. This scenario was repeated three times. He wore a one-piece garment with a black belt on the front of it. The Headmistress of their school asked the boys to write an account of what had occurred, but this has vanished.[42] Are we dealing here with one of the fairy tribe, an extraterrestrial or what? Who can tell? I can't.

In Somerset there seems to be a belief in a living patch of darkness which is pitch black. F. Hancock in 1897 saw a man in clear moonlight come on such a patch of darkness, which he struck with a stick.

One of the most horrible of frightening creatures is the Scottish nuckleavee. This ghastly creature lives in the sea, but has been known to come ashore. It is apparently skinless, you can see the red flesh inside its body, the black blood coursing through its yellow veins, it looks like a huge horse with flippers in place of legs and on its back is a human figure that seems to be part of the creature itself, not merely a rider, legless, but long armed. The creature has a huge mouth which voids steam-like breath and a single eye. The folklorist Walter Traill Dennison recounts what was supposedly an actual encounter with the creature by a man named Tammas, who happily escaped with his life. The animal bears some resemblance that the reader might find curious to the Fish-Knight, a fish that looked like a rider on a horse, who features in the *Parsifal* of Wolfram von Eschenbach.[43]

Other Scottish creatures of unpleasant intent are the Blue Men of the Minch. These are supposed to be water creatures found in the Minch, a stretch of water that divides the island containing Lewis and Harris from the mainland of Scotland. It has been said that these Blue Men symbolise the waves of the angry sea, but the Reverend John Gregorson Campbell, minister of Tiree from 1861 to 1891, met a man who claimed to have actually seen one, a man of blue colour with a long grey face in the sea, visible from the waist upwards.[44]

Another creature that seems to have caused alarm was the Illinois Monster. This was seen a number of times in 1972. It was described as 10'/3m tall and it looked like a cross between an ape and a caveman. Its face was long and grey and its mouth was red with sharp teeth. No one seems to have approached this creature closely enough to give it a friendly pat.

Let us venture back into history. The Newbury Demons allegedly plagued the settlers in Newbury (New Hampshire) in 1679. They slammed doors, broke windows and carried out other annoyance.

When settlers were settling in the Great Lakes region of North America, the Indians warned them about a decidedly hostile race of beings called the *Armouchiquois*. These were long-legged creatures and, around the 1700s, did everything they could to sabotage the settlement of their lands by whites. People who excited their anger suffered various minor ailments. However, one has a suspicion that they would have contracted these ailments anyway and the Armouchiquois were a convenient race onto which the blame could be cast.

In Lake Nuquisbum (Washington) the Bone-Cleaner is supposed to dwell. She looks like an old crone and eats anything she can get her hands on, excarnating it completely. The bones are clean indeed when she finishes with them.[45]

Another horror is *Letiche*. He is said to be a creature with wrinkled green skin. His eyes are said to be green and shining. His fingers and toes are webbed. Moss and gunk bedizen his face. He lurks in the bayous of Louisiana. He overturns boats to eat their occupants. One

---

43 M. Fleming *Not of this World* (Edinburgh, 2002), pp. 124-6
44 F. Thompson *The Supernatural Highlands* (Edinburgh, 1997), p. 103
45 W.H. Blackman *The Field Guide to North American Monsters* (New York, 1998), p.203

version of the story is he was raised by alligators and became part human, part alligator.

Crossing to England, we find the legend of *Black Annis,* a female who inspired horror. If you were travelling near Leicester, it would have been wise to avoid Black Annis's Bower, where, as you have probably guessed, Black Annis dwelt. Her face was blue and, if you felt the need to examine her fingernails, you would find them covered in human flesh. Children were warned about her, for it was said that when she captured them, she would suck out their blood and hang up their skins. What she did with their other organs does not seem to have been considered. She was also known as *Anna* or *Anny,* but *Annis* could have been the original of her name, a form, perhaps, of *Agnes.* In the 19th Century, it was believed she lived in a tunnel leading from the cellars of Leicester Castle to the Dane Hills. A festival at the Bower was held from long before 1668 (when it is first mentioned) to 1842 and it may be that Black Annis was a goddess in origin in whose honour these celebrations were originally held. She was sometimes referred to as *Cat Annis* and may have been a cat-goddess, her meat-encrusted fingernails having once been cat's claws. This is supported by the fact that the festival originally involved dragging a dead cat which was taken from the Bower to the house of the Mayor of Leicester, who must have been delighted to receive such a welcome gift. The dragging of the cat seems to have been discontinued in the 18th Century. The Dane Hills, where the Bower was, are now within the urban spread of Leicester.

Going north to Scotland, the *Finfolk* of Orkney and Shetland can be dangerous. They live in various realms called Hether Blether, Finfolkaheem and Hildaland. The men will sometimes abduct human wives and they do not treat them well. The females are mermaid-like, in that they have tails, but these tails are worn over their legs and can be removed. The females are dazzlingly beautiful for the first seven years, humanly beautiful for the second seven years and old crones for the third. But if they can procure a human husband, they keep their beauty, so they are always on the lookout for one. If she catches you and brings you to her underwater dwelling, she will mete out unpleasant treatment to you. If she goes to live with you ashore, she will presumably treat you rather better. The inhabitants of Orkney and Shetland are of Norse origin and the Norse applied the term *Finnr* to the Lapps or Saami. The Finfolk legend probably preserves a memory of early interaction with them.

A modern phenomenon, which seems to come from the United States, is the *stickman*. Often these look like a small child's drawings of men or they are very thin, as if each of their limbs and their body were formed by a single stick. I have no record of their having harmed anybody, but they are frightening to look at. One ran alongside a car and kept pace with it in Chaffee (Missouri) in 2003. It was of an aluminium shade and gangly in appearance.

A 7' tall creature, thin as a pencil with pointed joints, was seen in Manchester (Indiana) in 2004. A thin graphite individual was seen in Brazil the same year as was another stickman in Elkander (Iowa). On December 29th, 2011, in Kellyville (Oklahoma) a correspondent reading in bed saw a stick-like figure with bent arms and legs.

In 2004 a woman saw a creature looking like a stickman as she came towards her farmhouse in Eckander (Iowa). It turned its head and looked in her direction.

A correspondent of the *Fortean Times* website, walking at 6 a.m. and having taken neither drink nor drugs in Brockley, Lewisham, London, encountered a stickman coming towards him. He was accompanied by a friend, who also saw it. It was like a cardboard cutout and featureless. It advanced towards them and increased its speed, so they ran to the writer's house. From inside, they saw it come to the front door and apparently look through the glass. It then departed.

Professor Tolkien's barrow wights were based on a creature of North European legend, the *draug*. This was a living corpse which could leave its grave and was capable of shape shifting and weather control. It was not confined to the area of its burial. A draug drowned at sea looked like a human, except that its head was composed of seaweed. A somewhat similar creature was the *haugbui*, a living corpse buried in a mound. However, this had to stay on the site of its grave. This survives in Orkney as a friendly being called the *hogboon*.

The *afanc* is a creature that opposed and was slain by the hero Peredur in the Welsh *Mabinogion*. It used to live in a cave and kill its enemies with a poisoned spear. Depictions of this creature sometimes give the impression that it was some kind of animal, but few animals are able to cast spears. Another legend of this creature says it dwelt in a pool called Llyn yr Afanc on the River Conwy. A maiden lured it to her, so it fell asleep with its head in her lap. (This was a method supposedly used to capture unicorns, so it looks like a transfer of the story from animal to animal.) The afanc was bound in chains and it took two oxen to drag it out of the pool. Another afanc in Llyn Barfog was slain by King Arthur. There is a story of an afanc in Llyn Llion, but this is a late fabrication. The question that remains is, *What exactly was an afanc?*

The word was originally *avac*. It was confused with Welsh *afanc* (beaver). *Avac* has an equivalent word in Irish, *abhac*, which means a dwarf and it is probably this that the afanc originally was. Moreover, the root of *abhac* is *abh* (river) which would indicate a water-dwelling dwarf. Whether a real kind of creature lies behind the legend I cannot say, as I know of no modern reports.

It might be apposite to mention here *Sewerface*. He is not well-known, but falls within the scary category largely because he is not a lone humanoid, but is supposed to live in a sewer under Newtonbreda in Northern Ireland. Our only intimation of his existence is that he was allegedly picked up on CCTV. If I ever go on a rambling holiday in the sewers, I shall seek to avoid him.

Chapter Fourteen
Love and marriage

tHERE are sundry stories of mortals who married or had sexual relations with Otherworldly beings. The marriage stories seem to be largely variants on a theme, but, if there are fairies, such marriages might have occasionally taken place. There are even people accounted as being of fairy descent, though how fairies and humans, if they are essentially different, could interbreed might cause us to wrinkle our brows in speculation. As far as I know, no person of alleged fairy ancestry has undergone a DNA profile. Moreover, biologically, fairies and humans should belong to different genera, which is supposed to preclude interbreeding, according to received wisdom.[46] The same question would arise in which a human was supposed to have interbred with an extraterrestrial. In early heraldry, it was said that families claiming descent from fairies should have a leopard in their coats-of-arms. Thus the Dukes of Guienne had one, as they were supposedly descended from a fairy.

Fairy marriages seem to go wrong. We have already seen that they are surrounded with taboos, which are invariably broken. Thus the fairy is given accidental blows, accidentally touched with an iron bridle or fetter or stirrup. Yet these unions are not unblest with progeny. We have told of the Physicians of Myddfai and the Pellings. Families in Llandegai and Llanllechid used to be taunted because it is said they had fairy ancestry. I now intend to go back to the time of Walter Map (12th Century) to have a look at some early stories of the same type.

He tells us that fairies from a lake would emerge and dance in a field of oats, where they were espied by Gwestin of Gwestiniog. He captured one and married her, but she stipulated he should never strike her with a bridle (*probably because of the iron content*). She gave birth to many children, but eventually he struck her accidentally. He

---

46 Received wisdom is not always correct, however. African and Asian elephants belong to different genera and therefore should not be able to interbreed, but, as no one bothered to tell the elephants this, it has happened on one recorded occasion.

had to go out, but when he returned, he found her headed for the lake with her children. He was just in time to grab one called Trinio. Later, when Trinio fared badly in a battle, his mother took him beneath the waters of Brecknock Mere, where she dwelt.

Like the stories above, this one is in a Welsh setting; but Walter also has a story to tell set in England. The personage in this is Wild Edric, an historical character, who lived in the time of William the Conqueror. He flourished in 1068. In the forest one day he came on a house where he saw a number of tall women, taller than himself, but very beautiful, dancing. He rushed in and grabbed one, who had taken his fancy. She agreed to marry him, but on the grounds he never mentioned her sisters to her. He eventually did and she was gone.

These stories of fairy brides obviously go back a long way and we may ask if there is any truth behind them. I rather suspect that the lake was regarded as a fairy dwelling-place or portal to fairyland and the stories grew out of this. However, as I shall argue later, portals of some sort certain lakes may indeed have been and there may have been one actual incident on which the others were based. Incidentally, it has been suggested that the rumours of Edric's wife being a fairy may have sprung simply from her being very beautiful. The Weld-Blundell family claims descent from Edric – perhaps they have fairy blood? Edric in legend became a leader of the Wild Hunt, together with his fairy wife. There is a footpath in Shropshire called Wild Edric's Way – it stretches from Church Stretton to Ludlow.

A story from Smaland in Sweden tells how an elf maid entered a house through a knothole. She set up home with the householder and bore him four children, but eventually left him. We do not know why. Perhaps this is a form of the original account of such a union. It is interesting that, in these stories, the fairy bride always seems to have children.

Perhaps the most famous story of a fairy marriage that went awry is that of *Melusine*. The story has the hero Raymond meet a lady of outstanding beauty by a fountain in the woods. She consented to marry him, on condition that he never saw her on a Saturday. They had a number of children, but each had a physical defect. One Saturday, however, Raymond looked through the keyhole of the door of the bathroom to which she had retired and saw that she was half human and half serpent. Some time later, he chided her with this and she had to leave him, returning only at night to suckle her youngest children. She had built a castle named Lusinia and from this the Lusignan dynasty, who claimed descent from her, is said to have taken its name. Before the death of a Lusignan lord, Melusine was said to appear over the walls, wailing. Catherine de Medicis, Queen of France, was told by locals she was sometimes seen coming to bathe. Some said she appeared on the top of the Great Tower. Since the castle was destroyed, she was reputed to have come rarely.

The earliest Lusignan I can trace is Hugh I (10th Century) called *Venator*. There is no trace of Raymond here. However, one forms the impression that Raymond was supposed to be an ancestor of Hugh.

A variant of the story features the marriage of Melusine to Count Siegfried of the Ardennes.

Jean d'Arras in 1387 wrote a romance based on the story, but it was a piece of fiction, making Melusine the daughter of King Helmas of Scotland by a fairy named Pressina.

That a prominent family, which later was to supply the royal house of Cyprus, should claim this fairy ancestor is interesting, if no more than a legend. The sightings of Melusine by locals provides evidence of the latter's existence, but once again not proof. The locals who claimed to have seen her may have been deluded or mendacious.

Regarding less regular unions with fairies, the reader may remember that W.B. Yeats spoke of four or five people he knew who claimed to have had fairy lovers, while people claiming nereid descent were to be found in Greece. However, some such unions were not without their perils.

In Celtic mythology, the *leannán sí* is a fairy lover. If you do not succumb to her charms, she will be your slave. If, however, you do, you will waste away. She is found in Ireland, Scotland (as *leannan sith*) and the Isle of Man (as *lhiannan shee*).

On the male side, the Eskimo believe in a creature called the *uiirksak*. This is a creature described as a spiritual husband. Sometimes they have children by human women. Their female equivalent, the *nuliarksak* can have children by human males, but these men never see their offspring.[47]

The idea of an otherworldly lover is not confined to Celt and Eskimo. In the Middle Ages there was a considerable belief in incubus (male) and succubus (female). Their supposed attentions may sometimes be ascribed to sleep paralysis. This is a not uncommon condition which can occur when the sufferer is falling asleep or waking up. There is

---

47 I use the term *Eskimo* rather than *Inuit*, as not all Eskimos are Inuit.

the feeling that there is someone or something in the room and the sufferer is absolutely incapable of movement. The sufferer believes that some being is sitting on his chest and perhaps wishes to strangle him. It need not be an incubus or succubus – sometimes it is said to be a hag, having an out of the body experience. In Scandinavian lore the Mara, a female, will sit on person's chests and give them nightmares.

However, incubuses were sometimes believed capable of fathering offspring. According to Geoffrey of Monmouth, Merlin the wizard was the son of an incubus. Both incubus and succubus were said to apply their amorous attentions to unwilling victims. The offspring of an incubus and a human or of an incubus and a succubus is called a cambion.

On the island of Chiloé in Chile, a creature called a *trauco* is said to reside. Women cannot resist him and, if he makes one of them pregnant, because he is irresistible, no opprobrium is attached to the girl. One can see how this particular legend might have evolved. A trauco is 1'6"-2'6" in height.

South Africa boasts a being with various sexual associations called the *tokoloshe* (3 *syl.*). The penis of the tokoloshe is so long it has to fling it over its shoulder. It seems to have been a water spirit originally in the beliefs of the Xhosa, but is no longer found only there. It is not evil until a witch gets hold of it and makes it her familiar. Until then, it is not able to talk. The witch rewards it with food and milk. It can become invisible by putting a pebble in its mouth. It is said that people put bricks under their beds to avoid the creature's sexual attentions. In a blog by Dimago[48] he said he had been contacted by many people regarding their being troubled by the creature. In modern southern Africa it is a creature generally blamed for all kinds of misfortunes.

Is there anything real behind this being? In the 19th Century, Mrs M. Martin, whose husband was a British official in Lesotho, claimed she encountered a tokoloshe emerging from a cowshed. In 1916 Flora Nthshuntshe of De Aar, South Africa, saw a short being with a cape about his shoulders. His eyes shone.[49] In 1999 K.K. Manyika, Director of Security for the Zimbabwian Parliament, claimed he was attacked by a number of invisible tokoloshes. According to the *Daily Telegraph* website, a tokoloshe was causing trouble in the village of Bethanie, Nambia, in 2012.

---

48 www.tvsa.co.za December 1st, 2008
49 S.D. Tucker *Terror of the Tokoloshe* (Woolsery, 2013), p. 7.

It may be said in praise of tokoloshes that they like children and will not harm them.

Before leaving sexually-oriented and aggressive beings, mention must be made of one which does not seem to have been heard of until modern times. This is the *Popobawa*, which is sometimes reported with the wings of a bat, sometimes in other shapes. It seems to have been heard of for the first time about 1965 on the island of Pemba in Zanzibar, now part of Tanzania. It would attack adults at night, sodomising them. Belief in the creature spread throughout Zanzibar and then to Dar-es-Salaam on mainland Tanzania.

Belief in sexually active evil beings may be ascribed to various psychological causes rather than to real encounters. I shall merely mention that the one does not preclude the other. What exactly did Mrs Martin find emerging from her cowshed? What did Flora Nthshuntshe see?

Chapter Fifteen

mothman and the mothmen

a T THE beginning of this work I said it would not confine itself to fairies *strictu sensu*, but also to include various strange creatures reported from time to time. Such a one is the famous *Mothman* of West Virginia, a state which seems to be the locale of many a paranormal happening.

We must betake ourselves to Point Pleasant in that state, near which stood the TNT area. This is an area where many camouflaged buildings were erected in World War II to store explosives. The buildings are now bereft of camouflage and, one hopes, of explosives. There are many tunnels underneath the structure.

The first highly publicised sighting was that of the Scarberrys and Mallettes. These two couples were in a car driven by Roger Scarberry when they saw two bright red circles ahead – hypnotic eyes. Then they saw a man ahead of them, perhaps 7' tall, with a pair of wings folded against his back. Linda Scarberry said later that the creature definitely had human arms, which showed musculature, and human-like legs.[50] They drove away and the creature followed them to the town of Point Pleasant itself.

When word of this circulated, many cars went into the area next day, looking for the mysterious creature. Meanwhile a family called the Wamsleys and a Mrs Bennett saw, from a residence in the area, a 'big grey thing' rise up from the ground, as if it had been lying there. Mrs Bennett in fright dropped a baby she was holding, but it was unhurt. The party ran into the house as the figure began to unfold its wings. Two red eyes peered through the window.

On November 24th four people driving past the TNT area saw a giant flying creature with red eyes. On November 25th a humanoid unfolding its wings and taking off was seen by a startled Mr T. Ury. At least, I assume he was startled. The next day Mrs R. Foster, gazing onto

---

50 D. Sergeant and J. Wamsley *Mothman: the Facts Behind the Legend* (Point Pleasant, 2002), pp. 18-29

her front lawn, saw Mothman there and managed a look at its face. She saw no beak. This happened at St Albans (West Virginia). It was seen by Connie Carpenter near Mason in the same state on November 27th and, on the same day, in St Albans again by two children. The elder, Sheila Cain, said it was grey and white with big red eyes. It must have been 7' tall.

Although the Scarberry-Mallette sighting is the one which started Mothman fever going, there had been at least three other sightings – on September 1st, 1966, by a number of adults, who reported a man-shaped object in the sky at Scott (Mississippi); near Camp Conly Road, Point Pleasant, on November 1st, by a National Guardsman; and by five adults on November 12th.[51]

A couple of points may be mentioned here. If Linda Scarberry's testimony is accurate, there is no way this creature could have been a bird. Some books have stated it had no arms, thereby making a bird identification more plausible, but where they obtained their information is uncertain. Some large birds had been seen in the area and it may have resulted from confusion with those. In addition, Mrs Foster, who saw the face of the creature, did not discern a beak. With regard to the total number of witnesses, a figure of a hundred has been suggested, but queried; however, Linda Scarberry says she knew 30-40 people who had observed it, some of them more than once.

Connecting Point Pleasant to Gallipolis (Ohio) was a structure called the Silver Bridge. This collapsed on December 15th 1967, resulting in 46 deaths. The idea was mooted that there was some connection with Mothman. There seem to have been fewer sightings after the collapse, but no such connection has been established.

What people do not seem to realise is that there are many other reports of creatures that are similar to Mothman. In the 1900s at Point Pleasant itself and adjacent locations, reports were coming in of a *man-headed bird*. That one of the reports came from Looneyville should not be held against it. The *Texas Flier* was reported by two police officers in 1976 in San Benito, when a creature with a humanoid body flew over their car. The sighting of the *Tennessee Mothman* is undated, but the creature was observed by J. Quintero and his cousin. Creatures with batlike wings have been reported at The Gorge, an area in the vicinity of Akron (Ohio).

---

51 Coleman, L. *Mothman and Other Curious Encounters* (New York, 2002), p.172.

Batsquatch was supposedly encountered by Brian Carsfield in 1994 near Mount Rainier (Washington). This had gigantic wings and human-like hands (no mention of arms), a wolflike face and avian feet. The *Pennsylvania Mothman* was seen near Harrisburg in 2003. The *Manbat* of Wisconsin attacked a car driving along Briggs Road, Holden, in 2006. It had arms and legs with claws on the end of them and sharp teeth. Its wingspan was estimated at 10'-12'. A *Scottish Mothman* was reported in Edinburgh in 1992, perched on a branch. It was described as resembling a man and bird combination. A photograph of what may be a *German Mothman* is to be found on the Internet. It was taken by a tourist from York, who didn't see the creature when she took the picture. In the 1960s the *Virginia Mothman*, which had arms like wings, was seen in Haymarket (Virginia): there were four witnesses. The *Columbus Mothman* is said to have attacked a person in Columbus (Ohio) in 2003. The *Hollywood Mothman*, which was reported from Hollywood (Maryland) in 1944 was of huge size. The *Selma Mothman* was observed in Selma (Alabama) in 1948. The peculiar batlike creature seen in Van Meter (Iowa) in 1903 may be in the same category. No doubt other examples could be found. I am not for a moment saying all these creatures belong to the same species, but they cast doubt on any idea that Point Pleasant Mothman is one of a kind.

There is now a Mothman Festival held annually in Point Pleasant. This includes a Miss Mothman Pageant.

Mothman is not the only strange creature to be found in reports of the TNT area. In 1973 people driving in the vicinity noticed a creature gliding alongside them. It had shaggy hair, a huge head and seemed able to keep up with their car, which was travelling at 65 mph.[52] A white humanoid figure, big and wide, pursued people into their car in the same vicinity.[53]

Crossing the Atlantic, a strange flying creature has been reported from Cornwall. This is *Owlman*. The first sighting seems to be when Don Melling's daughters, June (12) and Vicky (9) perceived a horrible creature and ran to tell their father. The latter was informed that a certain "Doc" Shiels was in the area and, if one wanted to look into things anomalous, he might be a good person to start with. Shiels was a self-styled wizard and hoaxer and did not deny he played tricks from time to time, but he assured Melling he had nothing to do with this

---

52 *CFZ Yearbook 2013* (Woolsery, 2013), p.122
53 *Ibid.*

one. June drew a picture of the creature which showed an owl-like head, wings and a human-like body apparently covered with feathers.

On July 3rd there was a sighting by two girls called Sally Chapman and Barbara Perry of an owl-like figure that looked like a human.

Because of Shiels' eccentric history, suspicions were voiced that he had set the whole thing up, but he denied this.

Quite independent of all these sightings, two persons who were not in contact with Shiels and gave testimony uninfluenced by him, saw the Owlman in 1968. They preferred anonymity, so they were given the pseudonyms of Gavin Peabody and Sally Scollard. They said it was about 5' tall. It was grey and brown. The eyes glowed.

The eminent cryptozoologist Karl Shuker suggested they had seen an eagle owl (*Bubo bubo*). However, concerning this matter, it is safe to say that most mainstream zoologists didn't give a hoot.

A rather towering figure in cryptozoology, both physically and metaphorically, is Jonathan Downes, who had another idea. He felt the Owlman was perhaps a tulpa, which is a vibrant being projected by concentration, which in due course becomes independent of its originator. The tulpa forms part of the esoteric lore of Tibet. Alexandra David-Neel, a female convert to Buddhism, had claimed to have once produced such a creature in the form of a Buddhist abbot, which she had considerable difficulty in destroying when it started to turn nasty.

Leaving Owlman aside, another strange creature noted in Britain was the Hythe Mothman. Four teenagers, including John Coxton (17) and Mervyn Hutchinson (18) saw a star shooting into the sky at night. This resolved itself into the shape of a UFO. This occurred at Standing Park, Hythe (Kent) on November 16th, 1963. The UFO moved off through some woods. Then suddenly from the field over which it had been hovering, a creature came towards them. It had seemingly no head, wings like a bat's and was of adult human size. The teenagers ran off. Whenever creatures are asserted to have no head, I harbour the suspicion that they actually do have one, but they are holding it below the level of their shoulders, so it is not readily discernible. This creature seems rather different from the Mothman of Mount Pleasant, in that it had neither the red eyes nor the arms ascribed to that creature. Three peculiar footprints were found in the area on November 23rd, but whether they were connected with this strange apparition one cannot tell.

One point worthy of mention here is that wings the size of Mothman's would defy the laws of nature if used for flight. The musculature of Mothman is said to be insufficient for this. However, Mothman is generally described as gliding and that is probably their sole purpose. The other point worth mentioning is, despite whatever has been ascribed to other such creatures, Mothman himself does not seem to have harmed or tried to harm anyone.

As a postscript, I might mention another strange flying creature. Stan Gordon, a well-known investigator into the paranormal, reported this on February 9th, 2013, on the website *Paranormal News*. A couple in Washington County (Pennsylvania) reported a dark brown creature, standing upright, which had, apparently, glowing eyes. It took off in the sky. No wings were discernable. This occurred on April 13th, 2012.

Chapter Sixteen

the gift givers

THOSE who bring gifts to children include three well-known figures – Santa Claus/Father Christmas, the Easter Bunny and the Tooth Fairy. The purpose of this book is generally to show evidence of the objective truth of the entities it describes, but this chapter is an exception. The actual identities of the Gift Givers are known, but this is to give the interested reader some idea of the origins of their legends.

Santa Claus takes his name from St Nicholas, but the gift giver he has become has nothing particularly saintly about him. We actually know very little about Saint Nicholas, except that he was bishop of Myra (modern Mugla in Turkey) in the 4th Century. However, he has been widely venerated and is the patron saint of children. Thus in the Netherlands he gives gifts on the eve of his feast day, December 6th. He arrives by steamboat from Spain, clad in a red over-garment such as a chasuble. Riding a white-grey horse over the rooftops, he drops gifts down the chimneys.

A gift-giving character who is found amongst the Pennsylvania Dutch (who are in fact of German origin) is *Belsnickel* (wallop Nicholas) who wears a mask and has a long tongue.

Meanwhile, the practice of gift giving in Denmark involves a tomte, dressed in a red hat. He replaced the Yule Goat. Belief in him spread throughout Scandinavia and also to Finland, where he still retains the name of *Joulutonttu,* but dresses much like Santa Claus.

The actual term *Santa Claus* is first found in an American newspaper of 1773. The poem *The Night Before Christmas* (1823) attributed to C.C. Moore[54] gave him much the image he has today, but treats him as a diminutive being, like the Danish tomte. This poem also names his reindeer. The idea that he lived at the North Pole we may owe to the illustrator Thomas Nast, who also seems to have designed Santa's costume. In due course, Santa came to be thought of as being of human size.

---

54 There is some doubt about the authorship.

The curious idea that he had *flying reindeer* may have come from a Finnish source. They had a tradition that Old Man Winter flew about in a sleigh drawn by such beasts. This may go back to a shamanic practice. The ingestion of fly agaric mushrooms may give the illusion of flying, but they have unpleasant side effects. However, reindeer eat fly agaric and, if you drink reindeer urine, you find the whole hallucinogenic experience more congenial. This may reflect shamanistic practice.

Meanwhile, in England the idea of *Father Christmas* had grown up. He was depicted as long bearded and wearing green. Many trace him to the god Odin/Woden and the Winter Solstice, but he is not mentioned before the 15th Century. This would leave rather a long time between the era when Woden/Odin was worshipped by the Anglo-Saxons or Vikings and his first appearance. He came to preside at mumming plays. These curious performances, given usually at Christmas, one would think might have been originally fertility rites, but there are two objections to this. The first is that all manuscripts we have of them are in standard English, whereas, if they were genuine rustic survivals, one would expect them to be in dialect. The second is the silence of antiquarians about their existence.

Father Christmas and Santa Claus were to become fused into a single character. The term Santa Claus seems to have reached Britain in the 1870s. At about the same time, people began to see Father Christmas as a gift bringer for children. In modern times, the terms are used interchangeably in Britain. (There may be some grumbles about this. For example, in the television soap opera *Coronation Street*, Percy Sugden in one episode insists he is playing Father Christmas, not Santa Claus, on the grounds that Santa Claus was imported from America.) He is said to enter by the chimney and this is one of the traits whereby he might be identified with Woden/Odin, who did likewise. The custom of hanging up stockings may be quite old, at least in the north of England.

In the United States, he is sometimes referred to as *Kris Kringle*. This is because of German influence. In certain German-speaking areas of Europe, the Gift Bringer is the *Christkindl*, originally intended to represent the baby Jesus, now sometimes an angelic spirit, usually played by a teenage girl. Thus *Kris Kringle's Book* was published in 1842, while *Kris Kringle's Christmas Tree* saw print in 1845.

The reindeer of Santa Claus have been replaced by white kangaroos in Australia, no doubt to accommodate the character to the local scene.

In other countries, the Gift Bringer varies. In Spain, gifts are brought by the *Magi*. The Basques have *Olentzero*, said to be the only giant who accepted Christianity. *Befana* in Italy is said to leave gifts as she looks for the baby Jesus. In Russia *Ded Moroz* appears at New Year celebrations, the Communists having tried to quell his associations with Christmas. He has a long coat. He is also known in the Ukraine and Belarus. He is accompanied by his granddaughter *Snegurochka* (snow maiden). At Epiphany in New Brunswick *Mother Goody* turns up bearing presents.

In some countries the Gift Bringer has a companion. The *Krampus* of Central Europe punishes wicked children. His name means "the clawed one", but he has a goat's horns and hooves. He is a quite terrifying creature. *Knecht Ruprecht* is a kind of Wildman, and is sometimes the Gift Giver himself. In the Netherlands, *Zwarte Piet* who comes with St Nicholas is a blackened Moor.

The persona of Father Christmas in mumming plays was accompanied by two beings whose function is not clear. One is *Niddy-Noddy*, all head but no body, who seems to have been a man in a large head with his feet sticking out at the base. Another is *Mary Tinker,* a woman played by a man.

The tradition of a visitor or gift bringer at the winter solstice in pagan times must have been a custom that was perhaps limited to northern Europe, but has spread over the centuries.

The Easter Bunny may have, in origin, not been associated with Easter itself, but with spring. It is first found in Germany and began as a Lutheran idea, but has since spread more widely. The Pennsylvania Dutch brought it to the United States as the *Osterhase* (Easter Hare). In parts of Europe it still retains its leporine character. In English-speaking countries it is generally seen as a rabbit. Its function is to provide Easter eggs.

My son Kieran, in his youthful days, rushed home from school one day to announce, "I know who the Tooth Fairy is!" He went on to elaborate, "It's Daniel Thompson's father." Daniel Thompson's father, I can assure the reader, has nothing reminiscent of a fairy about him, but Daniel had seen him replace a tooth with a coin and jumped to conclusions concerning his father's unguessed identity.

Just when the idea that fairies collected teeth arose is rather uncertain. Their store of teeth is, however, mentioned by the poet Robert Herrick (1591-1674).

The Spanish writer Luis Coloma, using perhaps a folklore character, produced a book called *Ratoncito Perez* (1894) which dealt with a mouse who collected children's teeth. In France, tooth fairies are seen as mice. In England, the belief in tooth fairies was established by the 1920s. Whether Coloma's book, which was translated into English in 1915, had anything to do with this is another matter. In Lowland Scotland an equivalent of the Tooth Fairy is called the White Fairy Rat.

The origins of these gift givers will, I hope, be of interest to the reader, even those that flourish only in the reality of believers. I should add that Daniel Thompson's father should not be approached with quantities of teeth by those seeking remuneration.

Chapter Seventeen
what and whence

HAVE we, with all these anecdotes of reported sightings and interaction, proved the existence of fairies and otherworldly folk associated with them? I am the first to admit we have not. Despite the large number of tales, to which I feel I might add considerably had I but the leisure, we cannot make the proud claim that we have proved the existence of the creatures described in them. Every one of these accounts might have been voiced by liars, people whose memories had beguiled them, people who made mistaken observations, raving lunatics and people who were fed false information. However, there is a kind of cumulative evidence. It is most unlikely that all or even the majority of the accounts mentioned above are false. The *balance of probability* is that some, perhaps the majority, are true. Therefore, although we have not proved these creatures exist, we have demonstrated the *likelihood* of their existence. This is the best we can do with the evidence available. To assert more would be dishonest.

But, if these creatures exist, where are they for most of the time? We can hardly claim that we bump into them as we walk the city streets, the country lanes or the bosky paths. It almost seems as if they are there, but are not *always* there. The idea of a part-time existence seems, on the face of it, absurd.

A number of less orthodox writers have tried to find explanations for the accounts of otherworldly beings without shedding science. D. Ash and P. Hewitt[55] have produced an interesting idea, but one which would not, I feel, commend itself to the vast majority of scientists. They argue that each basic particle of matter is, in fact, not something solid, but a vortex. They argue that energy is to be equated with movement and they disparage the physicists for not saying what exactly energy is. They feel there is a possibility, though, that movement can go faster than light.

---

55 D. Ash and P. Hewitt *Science of the Gods* (Bath, 1990).

This last assertion would probably be rejected utterly by most physicists. Since Einstein produced his Special Theory of Relativity in 1905 stating that nothing in the universe can outspeed light, this has become something analogous to a religious dogma among physicists. In case you are wondering, the speed of light is 299,792,458 metres per second. However Ash and Hewitt aver that scientists used to claim that sound could not be outsped and it now has. They ask if Einstein could have been wrong.

They continue that if movement could outspeed light and was identical with energy, it would produce super-energy. Matter composed of super-energy would not interact with things in our world and light would not reflect off them. *Bodies of super-energy* would be outside space and time. The light barrier would be the line dividing the physical from the super-physical. When a body went through the barrier, its atomic and molecular structure would not change. The Super Physical Realm would not be accessible by space and time.

As Ash and Hewitt are both science graduates, the first from London, the second from Cambridge, we must assume that, however heretical their propositions may seem, they have some idea of what they are talking about. As I interpret their theory, they are saying that, while you can't walk to the Super Physical Realm, your body's energy might be brought into it and then sent back, after the fashion of supposed fairy abductions; and that similarly beings in that world might be able to alter their movement speed and enter our space-time continuum as fairies (not to mention aliens) are said to do. The only way to enter the Otherworld, however, would be if you were moving at a speed greater than that of light.

Not being myself a scientist, I hope I have been fair to Ash and Hewitt's idea. It is a possible explanation for tales of an Otherworld which has at times been penetrated by beings from our own. It would explain accounts of people who suddenly vanish. (There is a particular account of one of these in Ron Quinn's book.) If we regard it as a theory, a possibility, but no more than that, we are doing it justice, but I do not feel Ash and Hewitt have given absolute proof of their argument.

However, if we are to sustain an argument that fairies might exist, the idea of there being an Otherworld in which they dwelt would be very useful to us. What exactly, though, would an Otherworld be? I am not sure we have the necessary vocabulary to delineate the concept, so I am going to try to explain it by analogy. Imagine there is an athletics event taking place. A series of tracks is laid out, one beside the other. Imagine that there isn't just one, but a series of universes, all laid alongside each other. Imagine further that there are barriers between each, so that you cannot just walk from one to another. By *you* I mean any specimen of *Homo sapiens* perusing this book. But there may be some beings, of a different nature to us who can gain ingress to our universe and egress from it. That would solve the problem of where fairy beings and other creatures many consign to the dustheap of myth may come from and go to.

There may be any number of such universes, with different creatures in each. This would mean there is a multiverse, a term I first encountered in the science fantasy novels of Michael Moorcock, but which I gather has now achieved a certain respectability in the scientific community. There is one facet where the athletics analogy does not work, however. If you are on track A, you cannot reach track C without crossing through track B. However, theoretically, if you once learn how to go from one universe to another, it may be possible to fare directly into any universe without crossing any intermediate ones. This means that fairy realms such as Avalon might be reached by crossing into another universe.

But hold once more! I hear a cautious reader cry. *Whatever about theoretical other universes, we have no jot of evidence that they're there at all. Why should they be there? Explain in no fewer than 500 words.*

It is now the general consensus amongst scientists that our universe was started with a *Big Bang*. The originator of this phrase was the astronomer Sir Fred Hoyle, who didn't believe in it. Astronomers today take a different view. There was a tiny amount of matter that went boom. I am now going to invoke what is known as the WMAP. This is an acronym for the Wilkinson Microwave Anistropy Probe. (Scientists, in their definitions, love using long words like Wilkinson.) This was a satellite able to photograph the universe at a young age and we now know the Big Bang took place 13.7 trillion years ago. This has given rise to an inflationary theory of the universe. The universe expanded greatly after the Big Bang and continues to expand and this may well lead to other big bangs, producing co-existing universes. Indeed, our own universe may have come into existence as a result of a big bang caused by the expansion of a pre-existing universe. There may be an immense number of universes out there and they may be continuing to produce further universes which in their turn will produce even more.

Scientists are even now debating whether it will be possible to enter them. But this does not mean they are at vast distances from us in the sense that any journey thither would involve years of travel. If we find a mode of ingress, we should be able to merely step into them. Such modes of ingress might be through simple portals and there is evidence that such portals do in fact exist. These portals would equate to the modern scientific concept of *wormholes*. Scientists maintain that through *Lorentzian Traversable Wormholes* (if they exist) it may be possible to visit distant planets light years away or to penetrate other universes.

One of the chief arguments in favour of this is the argument of *time*. A different universe would presumably run at a different time from ours. Tales of fairy abductions are found in which a human is taken into the fairy realm and is returned after a short time there to find many years have passed on earth. The way this is expressed in fairy tales is generally "He thought only a short time had passed, but when he returned he found many years, even centuries, had passed". In fact, this is the only way primitive people could express the idea, but my guess is that only a short time had passed, but the protagonist had been returned far further along our space-time continuum. I know of no tales, mind you, of anyone being returned to earth at a time *before* he entered Faerie. But such might account for reports of people seeing doppelgangers of themselves.

It might be appropriate to include one or two legends of this sort here. A man disappeared in Wales when looking after his cattle. He played his flute for a number of little men. He returned home thinking three hours had passed: in fact, it had been about three years.[56] A Chinese book written by Tu Kuang-t'ing (850-933) spoke of a man who visited an Otherworld for a short time only to discover on his return that nine generations had passed. One of the Saami, who took refuge in a witch's house, found when he escaped that, instead of spending only a night there, he had tarried six months. Hartland notes that near Bridgend was a house said to have once been occupied by a woman who left it and returned after ten years, thinking she had been away but ten minutes. At the village of Kolomenskoye in Russia, wildmen had been observed since 1556. The local belief was they came through a portal in a gully called Golosovyi. A story claimed that in 1825 two men entered the portal. A Wildman helped them to return

---

56 E.S. Hartland *The Science of Fairy Tales* (London, 1891), pp. 166-7.

and, although they had been gone for only a day, twenty years had elapsed since their departure.

In sum, the realm or realms of the fairies would exist on the far side of the universal boundary. This would account for the fact that fairies and similar creatures seem to be in our world some of the time, but not all of it. It would account for the fact that bones of fairies are rarely if ever found. It accounts for the scarcity of fairy artefacts, homes and remains. It might even account for the fact that in some places where a population of hominids could not survive in secret, they are occasionally seen.

Are there any reports of people or beings coming through the dimensional barrier? A number of accounts might suggest this. However, from a scientific point of view, they have the drawback of being anecdotal. Take, for example, the famous Skinwalker Ranch in Uintah County, Utah. This place, officially known as the Sherman Ranch, had a great many anomalies associated with it. It was eventually bought by the National Institute of Discovery Sciences. An investigation into the phenomena was undertaken by Dr Colm Kelleher and his team. They used scientific methods in their investigations. The phenomena had been reported by the Gorman family, which had acquired the ranch. They included orbs of light, mutilation and disappearance of cattle and the appearance of what are described as otherworldly creatures. However, what interests us particularly here is a sighting which took place before the scientific investigation commenced. Tom Gordon, the father of the family, noticed an orange object in the night sky. He had seen it on a number of previous occasions, always at the same place. He looked into the orange object and it was like looking into a window, with another sky on the other side. He judged it was about a mile away and through it he could see another world or time. Although it was night in this world, there was a blue sky at the other side of the object. Another night when the object appeared he trained a night vision scope on it. This time, he didn't see the blue sky, possibly because it was obscured by a black figure coming through the object. It was a black triangular object and it flew out of the orange frame. Tom Gorman had apparently seen a triangular craft fly out of another universe or dimension into this one.[57]

Nicholas Mann feels there is what he calls an Avalon Soul Portal on Glastonbury Tor in Somerset.

57 C. Kelleher/G. Knapp *Hunt for the Skinwalker* (New York, 2005), pp.62-64

Ron Quinn, in his fascinating book on sightings of Little People in the Catskill Mountains, tells of an incident which occurred at the Neversink Reservoir. The protagonist of this tale is identified only by the name Dave – those who supply accounts of paranormal experience often need the cloak of anonymity to spare them from ridicule. When Dave had been walking by the reservoir for some time, he noticed a bank of fog over the lake water. Then he came to a bridge which led into the fog. He found that the bridge appeared strange: it might have been made of brass and there were strange symbols on it. He walked across it into the fog and found himself on a small, befogged island, whose area he put at six acres. The trees were strange looking and there were strange animals in the offing. He saw three men wearing white robes, with silky hair running down their backs. They were bearded and had white robes. They looked as though they were scrutinising the far bank of the lake through the mist, which here at least was not so dense. One carried an object, which Dave could not make out. One of them turned around, but didn't seem to see Dave. All of this made Dave feel somewhat uneasy and he retraced his steps across the bridge. Both the bridge and the fog disappeared, but, apparently only for a moment, he saw on the far side of the lake a mountain which shouldn't have been there. The anomalous mountain vanished. The island disappeared too, but at what stage in the sequence it vanished or whether Dave actually saw it vanishing is not made clear.

A similar tale is set in the state of Washington. A doctor was walking by the lake, which was misty. He came on a bridge leading to an island in the mist. Strange animals were there, as was a single man, well stricken in years. It slowly vanished, presumably after the doctor had returned to the lakeside.[58]

Janet Bord has two accounts of apparent entries to otherworlds, both taken from *Fate Magazine*. The first concerns two children from Flackton (Arkansas) and took place in the 1920s. They were headed for a baseball game and went through the woods. They came to a stream they had never seen before and, when they crossed it, they seemed to be in a different world altogether. The plants were unrecognisable, some looking like giant ferns, and they saw a bird they could not identify. They went in the direction of the baseball ground and eventually saw it in the distance, as though they were watching it on a stage. They retraced their steps and recrossed the stream. When they looked back,

---

58 R. Quinn *Little People* (Lakeville, 2006), pp. 65-67.

the mysterious world had gone. They do not state if the stream was still there. Interestingly, the narrator (one of the children) said that their state of mind was one of *languor*. This I include, because it may be relevant to their state of consciousness during the experience.

Mrs Bord's second account concerns two hunters, nephew and uncle, in New York state in 1962. It was snowing and the snow on the ground was thick. To get past some pines, they had to penetrate underbrush. Having done so, they found they were in a place where the pines were in straight rows, 500 yards long and 300 yards wide. The sun was shining at the far end of this expanse. Looking backward, the narrator could see the way by which they had entered and the snowy weather on the other side of it. Within the pines the snow was merely about 2" deep. The narrator went through some underbrush at the end of the area and discovered himself in a place 3-5 acres in extent, where the grass was green, the birds were singing and flowers were blooming, with a hot temperature. They dozed in the sunshine for about three quarters of an hour. Then they decided to return to their car, where others of their party were waiting. As they retraced their steps, they made sure the tracks remained visible. They led the narrator's father and another uncle back, but, although they reached the location of their strange experience, the weather in which they had sunbathed was completely gone.[59] This does not appear to be entry into some otherworld, but more like a temporal anomaly, in which they entered the area at some other time of the year, or even a meteorological anomaly.

If you go to Annaton (Wisconsin), it is said locally that from time to time a sort of doorway appears on the side of the bluffs. When you look through it, it appears to be a different scenario or time on the other side.[60]

Elizabeth Goudge, the novelist, wrote a children's book called *Linnets and Valerians* (1964). At the end of it she included an Epilogue, in which she gave some details of writing it. She told of a friend who had a very unusual experience. She was driving over Dartmoor one evening and suddenly found herself in a wonderful wood, which she had never seen before. In due course she came to her house. In the morning, the wood had completely vanished. However, an old moorman knew all about the wood. He told her she would never see it again, it only happened once in a lifetime.

---

59 J. Bord *Fairies* (London, 1997), pp. 144-5.
60 C. Lewis, N. Voss and C.L. Nelson *The Van Meter Visitor* (Eau Claire, 2013), p. 72.

Whether these people entered other dimensions, worlds or times I do not know. But their experiences, if true, do indicate that there are realms with which we lack general acquaintance.

We have many reports and an even greater number of legends and stories of fairies, little people and other strange creatures; we can explain how they might have an impermanent presence on this planet; and we can explain where they might go, when not here. I feel we have demonstrated the possibility and even probability of some of these races' existence. More with the evidence to hand I do not claim; but the position established here may stir some imaginative souls to seek out greater evidence and actual proof.

Appendix One
faiRy beings mentioneb by name

Morgan La Fée

Although in later romances she was Arthur's foe, in earlier works she was a benevolent character and in the *Vita Merlini* of Geoffrey of Monmouth she took Arthur to Avalon after his final battle, to be healed of his wounds. The Welsh called her *Modron* and she seems to have been in origin a goddess, daughter of the ancestor-deity *Afallach*. Legend says she bore twins to King Urien of Rheged, an historical ruler of the 6th Century. It is widely thought that she was a later form of the Celtic goddess *Matrona*. The idea that she was Arthur's sister may stem from a remark in *Erec et Enide* by Chrétien de Troyes.

Matrona had a son called Maponos, who appears in Welsh literature as Mabon son of Modron. He surfaces again as Mabuz in the *Lanzelet* of Ulrich von Zatzhikoven where he is the son of the Lady of the Lake. This means that Morgan was the (or at least a) Lady of the Lake.

Velebitska Vila

An important vila who is said to dwell in the Velebit Mountains of Croatia.

Áine

An important Irish fairy, who was said to occupy Knockainy in County Limerick. She was the supposed ancestor of the Eoghanacht dynasty which ruled Munster in early times. In later medieval times the Geraldines, the Norman earls of Desmond, numbered Áine as one of their ancestors in popular folklore. Earl Maurice (1331-1390) was said to be the father by her of Earl Gerard (1390-1432). It is said that Earl Gerald is still beneath Lough Gur and every seven years he is seen riding a white horse. At midsummer it was the custom of the people to carry bunches of straw to Knockainey and it was said Áine sometimes appeared on the hill.

Gwydion

This was one of the kings of the Welsh fairies, his consort being Queen Gwenhidw. He was originally a god of the ancient Britons, as is shown by his being referred to as the son of the goddess Dôn. He is credited with making the Milky Way, called *Caer Gwydion* in Welsh. Despite all this, one tradition says he died and was buried near Caernarfon. His son was called *Huan*, which means the sun, which would indicate that he was once revered as a deity.

Gwyn

One of the kings of the Welsh fairies, he was reputed to live at Drum on the River Tawe. He is a Celtic god in origin, the son of Nudd (anciently Nodens). His domain was actually in Annwn. He would hunt with a pack of hounds, the Cwm Annwn, but the notion that he sought souls is mistaken. He had a horse called Carngwn and a red-nosed dog named Domerch. This strange animal had a tail with fan-like ends instead of back legs. He derives from the Celtic god Vindos, who gave his name to Vienna (anciently *Vindobona*) and other places.

Finvarra

The king of the fairies of Connacht (the western province of Ireland). He is supposed to rule from Knockmaa in County Galway. He is probably a folk version of Finbar, a member of the Tuatha Dé Danaan. His wife is variously said to be called Nuala or Úna.

Mab

A fairy queen first mentioned by Shakespeare. She is referred to a number of times in English literature and is called the fairies' midwife. She is supposed to rule a realm beneath Northumberland. In size she is tiny.

Oberon

The King of the Fairies in Shakespeare's *A Midsummer Night's Dream*, he supposedly is in origin a dwarf called Alberich in the German poem *Otnit*. He appeared in various pieces of medieval literature, notably *Huon de Bordeaux*. He was said to be the father of Robin Goodfellow/Puck.

Diana

Diana was originally revered as a goddess, perhaps the consort of a god named Virbius. J.G. Fraser thought her identical in origin with the Roman goddess Juno. In modern folklore she has been regarded as queen of the fairies.

Titania

The name of Oberon's queen in *A Midsummer Night's Dream,* it seems to be an invention of Shakespeare, taking it from the word *Titan,* one of the gods in Ancient Greece who were replaced by the Olympians.

Goldemar

Goldemar or Vollmar was a king of the dwarfs. Some account of his activities may be found in the chapter entitled 'Fairy Artefacts'. He had long silver hair and was an accomplished harper. He lived for a time at Castle Hardenstein.

Rumpelstiltskin

We first hear of this worthy in a tale by the Brothers Grimm. His name means 'little rattling post'. He is the villain of a tale in which he helps a damsel spin straw into gold in return for her first child. The tale has a wide number of variants throughout Europe. In the English version he is called *Tom-Tit-Tot.* In the Aarne-Thompson folktale classification, this is type 500.

Laurin

A dwarf king who ruled in the Dolomites and who abducted the Princess Similde, but she was rescued in a rose-garden. Laurin tried to escape wearing his cloak of invisibility, but the roses through which he ran showed where he was going, so he cursed them, so they could not be seen by day or night. However, they are visible at twilight. This phenomenon is called the *Alpenglow.*

Doamna Zinels

A Romanian fairy queen, she was the patroness of a secret society called the *Calusari,* who performed a strange acrobatic dance. Although they had a fairy queen as their titular head, the organisation admitted men only.

Wayland Smith

Called in Norse *Volundr*, he was at least at times regarded as an elf rather than a human. He seems also to have at times been regarded as a giant. King Nidudr, an unscrupulous monarch, procured Wayland's services and lamed him so he could not escape. To pay him back, Wayland killed his sons and raped his daughter, then escaped. The daughter bore Wayland a son called Widia. Wayland had a handy brother called Egil, who made wings for him with which to accomplish his escape. The Anglo-Saxons brought Wayland to England, where a megalithic tomb was declared to be his smithy. The legend that Wayland worked there as an invisible smith persisted at least until the 19th Century.

Dziwitza

A beautiful fairy princess and huntress in the folklore of Poland. The word is sometimes used as a plural noun. When there is a plurality of *dziwitzas*, it is believed they will sometimes rape men.

Basa Jaun

Basa Jaun is a being of Basque belief. He is sometimes regarded as an individual, sometimes as a species. Basa Jaun is said to be strong, dangerous and hairy. His wife is called Basa Andre. There is a female equivalent of Basa Jaun called Zuberoa, but she is distinct from Basa Andre.

Ravijojla

A vila in a tale of Prince Marko, the Serbian and Bulgarian hero. She helped him to kill Musa the Outlaw, who had three hearts.

Jerisavlja

Leader of the fairies known as vilas in Serbian folklore.

Ghille Dubh

This being supposedly lives in the Scottish mountains. He dresses in leaves and moss and will lead home children who have become lost. There was supposedly a sighting during the 18th Century.

Ana

The name of the Queen of the Fairies in Romany Gypsy lore.

Hedley Kow

Shapeshifting being of the north of England.

Ileana Cosanzeana

Dazzlingly beautiful Romanian fairy princess who married the knight Fat-Frumos.

Nicnevin

Scottish fairy queen, perhaps based on Scathach, goddess of the Isle of Skye.

Cliona

Irish fairy, said to live in an underground palace. She was known at times as the Queen of the Fairies of Munster (the southern province of Ireland). One legend makes her the daughter of Manannan the sea-god and she is supposed to have been drowned, which would indicate that in original mythology she was a sea-goddess.

Teramo

A spirit of Italian folklore, he seems to be descended from *Turms*, an Etruscan god. He was regarded as a protector of thieves, provided the thieves concerned did not shed blood and gave some of their goods to the poor. He also seems to have been a patron of merchants.

Habundia

Queen of fairies, witches and harpies in medieval lore.

Peg Powler

A spirit of the River Tees in England, who was of a murderous nature. It is possible she was a goddess in origin to whom sacrifices were offered, but it is also possible she was invented to keep children away from river banks.

Dahut

In Breton legend, the daughter of King Gradlon of Cornouaille. She let the sea overwhelm the city of Ys and was cast into the ocean and became a morgan, a kind of female water spirit with legs rather than a fishtail. In 1837 she was wrongly identified with *Ahes*, an old woman of Breton legend.

Tinia

This was the name of the chief god of the Etruscans. In later Italian folklore, he became a spirit, associated with thunder, lightning and hail.

Kalo

The Queen of the Mountains in modern Greek folklore. She is a nereid leading followers through her domain.

Tago

The ancient Etruscans had a peculiar god called Tages, who, when ploughing was in progress, sprang from the earth with the body of a baby but the wisdom of an old man. He seems to be the origin of the Italian fairy Tago, called 'the baby god'.

Tamara

A damsel who was cursed by her father and she became the River Tamar, which separates Cornwall from Devon. She was possibly in origin the river goddess.

Tiddy-Mun

Spirit of the Fens in the east of England, whose waters he was invoked to calm. He was depicted with white hair and a white beard. The Fens were watery marshland and Tiddy-Mun, who was regarded as a benevolent being in the area, was said to have sent a plague in response to their being drained. The locals dedicated another stretch of water to him. The Fens were also tenanted by goblin-like creatures called *tod-lowries*. (This term is used in Scots to mean a fox, but there is no evidence that it was so used here.) Another weird phenomenon was disembodied hands, which beckoned at the passing wayfarer. I would tend to avoid them, myself.

Lob Lie by the Fire

Also called a *lubber fiend*, he is a large, hairy home sprite, requiring payment in the form of a saucer of milk and the right to lie by a fire. He is endowed with a tail.

Tapio

In the folklore of Finland, king of the haltijas of the forest.

Tom Thumb

A traditional English folklore character, he is the hero of a story which first appeared in print in 1621. Thomas of the Mountain wanted a son and Merlin used his magic to bring this about, but the child was no bigger than a thumb. His various comic adventures include being swallowed by a cow, from which he has to exit by a way other than that by which he made his entrance. The German equivalent, *Thumbling*, is the hero of two stories from the collection of the Brothers Grimm. Perrault provides us with the story of the equally small Hop o' my Thumb (*Petit Poucet*).

Egeria

A nymph in Roman mythology, who may date from pre-Roman times. She was supposedly consulted by the legendary king Numa Pompilius, who is said to have reigned from BC 715-BC 673. She is also said to have dictated books to this monarch.

Ahti

In the folklore of Finland, the king of the haltijas who live in the sea.

Gronjette

A green giant in Danish folklore. However, his name may originally have signified 'beard giant'.

Appendix Two
a gLossary of european fairy species

For those wishing to gain information on American Indian Little People, I can do no more than recommend the book by J. Roth, cited in the Bibliography.

Afanc: water-dwelling being, perhaps dwarfish, in Wales.
Aguane: female beings of human size (Italy).
Akka: female spirits of Saami/Lapps.
Aloja: female water spirit (Catalunya).
Ancho: friendly homesprite (Spain).
Anjana: good spirit (Cantabria).
Askafroa: guardian of the ash tree (Scandinavia, Germany).
Asrai: a kind of water fairy (England).
Bagan: spirit guarding farm animals (Slavic).
Bananach: battlefield-haunting female spirit (Ireland).
Bannik: spirit guarding bath house (Slavic).
Banshee: fairy woman who warns of approaching death (Ireland).
Barbegazi: dwarf with huge feet and long beard (Switzerland, France).
Barguest: spectre which can be of various shapes (England).
Bassadone: fairies, male and female, who blow kisses from the clouds (Italy).
Bean-nighe: otherworldly being washing the shrouds of those who will die (Scotland).
Bergelf: mountain elf (Germanic).
Berg-mönch: mine sprite (Germany).
Bibitte: spirit that resembles an umbrella; it swallows smoking adolescent boys (Brittany).
Biersal: diminutive cellar being (Germany).
Bilberry-man: evil and aggressive spirit (Germany).
Blud: evil spirit (Slavic).
Blue Men of the Minch: sea dwelling humanoids (Scotland).
Bluecap: mine spirit (England).
Bocai: a kind of fairy (Ireland).
Bocan: paranormal being (Scotland).

Bocanach: fairy who haunts battlefield (Ireland).

Bockmann: forest bogey (Germany).

Bodach: kind of bogey (Ireland, Scotland).

Boggart: homesprite in England.

Bogey, bogeyman: nursery creature used to frighten children.

Bogle: evil black being (Britain).

Boleguean: diminutive spirit living at tumulus (Brittany).

Bolotianyk: spirit dwelling in marsh (Slavic).

Boruta: spirit dwelling in fir tree (Poland).

Boudic, bouffon: diminutive being living on farm (Brittany).

Brownie: homesprite (Scotland, England).

Bwbach: home sprite that can be mischievous (Wales).

Bwca: fairy or ghost (Wales).

Callicantzaros: creature that can be any one of a number of shapes that appears in a crowd around Christmas (Greece).

Caoineag: wailing spirit who warns her clan of disaster (Scotland).

Capacaun: man-eating ogre (Romania).

Catez: creature half man half goat (Slavic).

Ceasg: freshwater mermaid, whose lower half is a salmon (Scotland).

Centaur: creature combining features of horse and man (Greece).

Church Grim: spirit that lives in a church (Northern Europe).

Cluricaun: diminutive being found in wine cellars (Ireland).

Coblynau: mine spirits (Wales).

Corn Buck: spirit of cornfield, a shape shifter (Germany).

Corrigan: diminutive being unfriendly to humans (Brittany).

Cyhyraeth: a spirit that moans before a death (Wales).

Dame Blanche: term applied to the White Ladies in France.

Dame Verte: tall, beautiful fairy dressed in green (France).

Derrick: this may be another name for the *pixy*.

Direach: deformed giant (Scotland).

Dirne-Weibel: female wood spirit (Germany).

Dobie: murderous Yorkshire sprite (England).

Domovoy: homesprite (Slavic).

Dooiney oie: being who warns farmers about oncoming storms (Isle of Man).

Draug: creature living in burial mound (Germanic).

Duende: homesprite; the term is sometimes more widely used (Hispanic).

Dunelf: mountain elf (Germanic).

Dunter: sprite occupying castles (Scotland).

Dusius: woodland sprite (Gaul).

Dvorovoi: farmstead spirit (Slavic).

Dwarf: diminutive being in Germanic myth and lore.

Earth-People: earth dwelling dwarfs (Germany).

Elf: diminutive being of Germanic mythology; Tolkien felt they were not always little.

Elfin: female elf.

Ellylon: ugly small being (Wales).

Fachan: being with hand protruding from chest (Scotland).

Fadet, Farfadet: hair-covered subterranean dwarf (France).

Faun: being half man half goat (Ancient Rome).

Fear Clis: sky spirit (Scotland).

Fear Dearg: diminutive being, tricksy but not malevolent (Ireland).

Fenodyree: hairy humanoid, perhaps once a fairy knight (Isle of Man).

Filandière: human-sized beautiful fairy who spins (France).

Finz-Weibel: female being dwelling in woodland (Germany).

Fion: diminutive being (Brittany).

Flibbertigibbet: malevolent being (England).

Floriale: fairies who pollinate flowers in insect guise and vary in size from human to tiny (France).

Follet: fairy (France).

Folletto: Italian fairy.

Fuath: general term for dangerous supernatural being (Scotland).

Fujettu: mischievous being (Italy).

Fylgia: an attendant being on a child born with a caul (Iceland, Norway).

Galley-Beggar: being who carries head under arm (England).

Glaistig: used for various kinds of fairy; sometimes half woman, half goat (Scotland).

Glastyn: brownie, water horse or helper on farm (Isle of Man).

Gnome: diminutive being living underground.

Goblin: being of ugly appearance and diminutive size, usually malignant.

Gomme: mine sprite (France).

Goric: diminutive being found in megalithic structures (Brittany).

Gorska: mountain fairy (Bulgaria).

Grac'hed Oz: fairies resembling small old women (Brittany).

Grandinilo: diminutive being who causes hail (Italy).

Grant: fairy in equine form.

Gremlin: diminutive being who plays tricks in aeroplanes; the term is also used as an English equivalent for the African *tokoloshe*.

Gruagach: (1) long-haired female being (Scotland).
(2) giant or ogre (Ireland).

Grim: general name for an otherworldly creature.

Gryla: shaggy mountain fairy (Faroe Islands).

Guaxa: fairy of the Iberian peninsula, wild but graceful.

Gwyllion: fairies resembling old women (Wales).

Gwragged Annwn: water fairies (Wales).

Haltija: homesprite; also forest sprite or protecting sprite (Finland, Germany).

Hardmandle: short beings who live in hills (Switzerland).

Haugbui: living corpse buried in mound (Norse).

Heinzelmann: household sprite (Germany).

Hob: homesprite (England).

Hobgoblin: small being, often found in dairies, not malignant (England).

Hobthrust: homesprite (England).

Hobyah: disagreeable creatures, all eventually eaten by a dog, in American folklore.

Hogboon: benevolent creature living in burial mound (Orkney).

Hogfolk: beings between elves and humans (Scandinavia).

Holz-frau: female woodland creature (Germany).

Hooter: sea spirit (Cornwall).

Huldre-folk: elf-like beings (Iceland).

Iele: fairy race (Romania).

Judy: water fairy (Bulgaria).

Kannerez-noz: fearsome thin fairies of a dangerous nature (Brittany).

Katzenveit: malignant forest spirit (Germany).

Kelpie: dangerous equine spirit (Scotland).

Kerzel: diminutive mine spirit (Poland).

Keshalyi: good fairies (Romany).

Ketihaltija: home sprite (Finland).

Kikimora: female homesprite (Slavic).

Kilmoulis: mill spirit (Britain).

Kirnis: evil guardian of the cherry tree (Lithuania).

Klaubauf: horned and bearded sprite (Germany).

Klabautermann: water spirit dressed as sailor in Baltic Sea.

Klintkong: elf living on a cliff (Denmark).

Knocker: mine-sprite (Cornwall).

Kobold: homesprite (Germany).

Korrigan *v.* Corrigan.

Krasnal: diminutive being (Poland).

Lakanica: field spirit (Poland).

Lamia: beautiful female with duck's feet; also sometimes male (Basque).

Lamia of the Sea: female being who dances on the waves (Greece).

Lamiñak: sprite who says the opposite of what he intends (Basque).

Landelf: land elf (Germanic).

Lauru: male diminutive being with sexual proclivities (Italy).

Leprechaun: diminutive being in Irish folklore; now solitary, earlier gregarious.

Leshy: woodland spirit, resembling Wildman (Slavic).

Lisunka: female leshy (Slavic).

Longana: half woman, half goat (Italy).

Lutin: diminutive being (France).

Mamucca: small being who hides things in house (Italy).

Mara: nightmare spirit (Scandinavian).

Margot: beautiful but somewhat plump fairy, beautifully dressed (France).

Marte: strangely shaped kind of fairy with wide hips (France).

Mask: good-looking fairy who becomes ugly at night (Provence).

Massariol: small helpful being (Italy).

Meister Hammerling: mine sprite (Germany).

Menninkainen: diminutive forest spirit (Finland).

Mermaid: sea and lake dwelling female, half human, half fish.

Merman: male form of mermaid.

Metsik: forest spirit (Estonia).

Monacello: sprite dressed as monk (Italy).

Morgan: water spirit (Brittany).

Morozko: forest demon (Russia).

Mouro: subterranean being (Galicia, Asturias, Portugal).

Mumpoker: nursery bogle (England).

Muntelf: mountain elf (Germanic).

Muryan: shrinking diminutive being (Cornwall).

Nain: dwarf with catlike claws and hooves (Brittany).

Negret: small sprite (Majorca).

Nereid: in ancient Greece, a sea-nymph; in modern Greece, any kind of nymph.

Nickur: equine water spirit (Iceland).

Nis: homesprite (Norway, Denmark).

Niss-puk: home sprite (Germany).

Nix: water sprite (Germany).

Nixe: female of nix (Germany).

Norgg: small kind of ogre (Austria).

Nymph: ancient Greek female nature spirit.

Ogre: malevolent creature, sometimes gigantic.

Ojanacu: one-eyed giant (Spain).

Orcul: small kind of ogre (Italy).

Ork: malign spirit of mountains (Austria).

Pamarindo: unpleasant small being (Italy).
Pan: half man, half goat (Greece).
Pavaro: paranormal being with dog's head (Italy).
Pech(t): doughty diminutive sprite (Scotland).
Peilette: kind of marte (Belgium).
Pilwiz: fearful being that cuts corn (Germany).
Piru: forest demon (Finland).
Pixy: diminutive being (England).
Planetaros: Cypriot version of the *callicantzaros*.
Polevik: field spirit (Russia).
Pooka, Phooka: *v.* Púca.
Portune: diminutive being mentioned in Middle Ages.
Poulpiquet: valley diminutive sprite (Brittany).
Powrie: alternative name for dunter.
Psotnik: being who stirs up trouble (Slavic).
Púca: shape shifting being (Ireland).
Pwca: fairy that was possibly a home sprite in origin (Wales).
Redcap: alternative name for dunter.
Rusalka: beautiful water spirit (Slavic).
Salbanello: Italian sprite.
Salvanello: diminutive sprite (Italy).
Salvano: hairy being of human size (Italy).
Samodiva: powerful and beautiful female spirit (Slavic).
Satyr: in modern times regarded as part man, part goat; earlier regarded part man, part horse (Greece).
Scazzamurieddu: small sprite who wears red cap (Italy).
Schacht-Zwerg: mine sprite (Austria).
Scrattel: diminutive hairy being (Germany).
Sea-Trow: trow which dwells in the sea (Orkney).
Selkie: sea-dwelling human who disguises himself as a seal (Scotland, Ireland).
Shellycoat: evil river spirit (Britain).
Shisga: female kind of goblin (Russia).
Shumske Dekle: hairy female woodland dwellers (Croatia).
Silen: hominid with horse attributes (Ancient Greece).
Silvan: creature half man, half goat, larger than a faun (Ancient Rome).
Sinipiiat: female beings who care for flowers (Finland).
Skogsra: fairy who helped hunters and charcoal burners in return for sex (Sweden).
Small People: mine beings distinct from *knockers* (Cornwall).
Spriggan: nasty being, believed to be a giant's ghost (Cornwall).
Stille-Volk: earth-dwelling dwarfs (Germany).

Strömkarl: water sprite (Norway, Sweden).

Sumascazzo: Sardinian fairy.

Sylph: elemental of the air, according to Paracelsus.

Sylvester: spirit of the woods, according to Paracelsus.

Taterman: dangerous sprite (Germany).

Thusser: mound-dwellers (Norway).

Tommyknocker: American version of the Cornish *knocker*.

Tomte: a homesprite (Sweden).

Topielek: dangerous water spirit (Slavic).

Tornit: giant (Eskimo).

Trasgu: a homesprite (Spain).

Trenti: goblin of the woods (Cantabria).

Troll: (1) a giant (Norway, Sweden).
  (2) a diminutive being (Denmark).

Trow: diminutive being (Shetland, Orkney).

Truie de nuit: kind of marte (Belgium).

Tylwyth Teg: the Welsh fairies, given as being of varying height.

Ulk: elf-like being (northern Europe).

Vazila: spirit guarding horses; it has horse's ears and hooves (Slavic).

Ved: hairy being of human size (Croatia).

Vedenhaltia: water spirit (Finland).

Vesna: fairy with power over Fate and crops (Slovenia).

Vette: female wood spirit (Denmark).

Vila: female nature spirit (Slavic).

Vodyany: old fat ugly water spirit, male in gender (Slavic).

Waldgeister: wood spirit (Germany).

White Lady: human sized fairy clad in white; White Ladies are called *Weisse Frauen* in Germany and *Witte Wieven* in the Netherlands.

Wight: dwarfish supernatural being (Germany, England); the term *wight* can be used in English to mean a man.

Wildman: large hairy humanoid.

Witte-Juffern: cave-dwelling white ladies (Netherlands).

Wodewose: Anglo-Saxon Wildman.

Wolterkin: apparently a homesprite (Germany).

Xana: short fairy of caves and mountains (Asturias).

Zana: benevolent female spirit (Romania).

Bibliography

Abbott, G. *Macedonian Folklore* Cambridge, 1903.

Arnold, N. *Mystery Animals of the British Isles: London* Woolsery, 2011.

Arrowsmith, A. *A Field Guide to the Little People* London, 1977.

Ash, D./Hewiit, P. *Science of the Gods* Bath, 1990.

Baring-Gould, S. *A Book of Folklore* Pulborough, 1993.

Baring-Gould, S. *Curious Myths of the Middle Ages* London, 1894.

Bartrum, P.C. *A Welsh Classical Dictionary* Aberystwyth, 1993.

Benwell, G./Waugh, A. *Sea Enchantress* London, 1961.

Bergen, L./Delarose, S. *Ancient Aliens and Lost Islands* n.p., 2013.

Blackman, W.H. *The Field Guide to North American Monsters* New York, 1996.

Bord, J. *Fairies: Real Encounters with Little People* London, 1997.

Bord, J. *Fairy Sites* Glastonbury, 2004.

Briggs, K.M. *A Dictionary of Fairies* London, 1976.

Briggs, K.M. *The Anatomy of Puck* London, 1959.

Briggs, K.M. *The Fairies in Tradition and Literature* London, 1967.

Codd, D. *Mysterious Somerset and Bristol* Derby, 2011.

Coghlan, R. *Handbook of Fairies* Chieveley, 1998.

Coleman, L. *Curious Encounters* Boston, 1985.

Coleman, L. *Mothman and Other Curious Encounters* New York, 2002.

Colombo, J.R. *Mysterious Canada* Toronto, 1988.

Crossing, F. *Folklore and Legends of Dartmoor* Newton Abbot, 1997.

Dathen, J. *Somerset Fairies and Pixies* Milverton, 2010.

Downes, J. *The Owlman and Others* Exeter, 2001.

Doyle, A. Conan *The Coming of the Fairies* London, 1922.

Dubois, P. *The Great Encyclopedia of Fairies* London, 1999.

Eberhart, G.M. *Mysterious Creatures* Santa Barbara, 2002.

Evans-Wentz, W.Y. *The Fairy Faith in Celtic Countries* London, 1911.

Fairholt, F.W. *Gog and Magog* London, 1859.

Fleming, M. *Not of this World* Edinburgh, 2002.

Gregory, A. *Visions and Beliefs in the West of Ireland* London, 1920.

Grimm, J. *Teutonic Mythology* London, 1882-8.

Guiley, R.E. *Fairies* New York, 2010.

Hall, M./Coleman, L. *True Giants* San Antonio, 2010.

Hartland, E.S. *The Science of Fairy Tales* London, 1891.

Henderson, L./Cowan, E.J. *Scottish Fairy Belief* East Linton, 2001.

Henderson, W. *Notes on the Folk-Lore of the Northern Counties* London, 1879.

Hunt, R. *Popular Romances of the West of England* London, 1923.

Jones, A. *Dictionary of World Folklore* Edinburgh, 1995.

Jones, E. *A Relation of Apparitions of Spirits in the County of Monmouthshire and the Principality of Wales* Newport, Monmouthshire, 1813.

Jones, K.I. *Anne Jeffries and the Fairies* Penzance, 1996.

Kaku, M. *Parallel Worlds* New York, 2005.

Keel, J. *The Mothman Prophecies* New York, 1973.

Keightley, T. *The Fairy Mythology* London, 1850.

Kirk, R. *The Secret Common-Wealth* Cambridge, 1976.

Lawson, J.C. *Modern Greek Folklore and Ancient Greek Religion* Cambridge, 1910.

Leland, C.G. *Etruscan Roman Remains* London, 1892.

Lenihan, E. *Meeting the Other Crowd* Dublin, 2003.

Lewis, C. (et al.) *The Van Meter Visitor* Eau Claire, 2013.

MacKillop, J. *Dictionary of Celtic Mythology* Oxford, 1988.

MacManus, D. *The Middle Kingdom* London, 1959.

Markotic, V. (ed.) *The Sasquatch and Other Unknown Humanoids* Calgary, 1984.

Mullin, K. *This Wondrous Land* Chieveley, 1997.

Narvaez, P. (ed.) *The Good People* New York, 1991.

Newland, R. *Dark Dorset Fairies* n.p., 2008.

Nunnelly, B.M. *The Inhumanoids* Woolfathisworthy, 2011.

Ó hÓgáin, D. *The Lore of the Land* Cork, 2006.

Petry, M.J. *Herne the Hunter* Reading, 1972.

Porteous, A. *Forest Folklore* London, 1928.

Potts, M. *Mythology of the Mermaid and her Kin* Chieveley, 2000.

Quinn, R. *Little People* Lakeville, 2006.

Redfern, N./Vaudrey, G. *Mystery Animals of the British Isles: Staffordshire* Woolsery, 2013.

Rhys, J. *Celtic Folklore: Welsh and Manx* Oxford, 1901.

Rife, P. *America's Nightmare Monsters* San José, 2001.

Roney-Dougal, S. *The Faery Faith* London, 2003.

Roth, J. *American Elves* Jefferson, 1995.

Scot, R. *Discoverie of Witchcraft* London, 1584.

Sergent, G./Wamsley, J. *Mothman: the Facts Behind the Legend.* Point Pleasant, 2002.

Simpson, J./Roud, S. *Dictionary of English Folklore* Oxford, 2000.

Sinistrari, L. *Demoniality* Paris, 1879.

Smith, M. *Bunyips and Bigfoots* Alexandria (N.S.W.), 1996.

Spence, L. *The Fairy Tradition in Britain* London, 1948.

Steiger, B. *Out of the Dark* New York, 2001.

Thomas, L. *The Natural History of Trolls* (lecture typescript).

Thomas, L. *Weird Waters* Woolsery, 2011.

Thompson, F. *The Supernatural Highlands* Edinburgh, 1997.

Thorpe, B. *Northern Mythology* London, 1851-2.

Tomkinson, J.L. *Haunted Greece* Athens, 2004.

Tucker, S.D. *Terror of the Tokoloshe* Woolsery, 2013.

Varner, G.R. *The Folklore of Faeries, Elves and Little People* n.p., 2012.

Waldron, G. *A Description of the Isle of Man* London, 1744.

Westwood, J. *Albion* London, 1985.

index

www.ingramcontent.com/pod-product-compliance
Lightning Source LLC
Chambersburg PA
CBHW031513270326
41930CB00006B/388